Excerpts from unsolicit
In Christ Ministries fro
this series:

MW00364440

I can truly say that, after finding Jesus as my Saviour, entering into the fullness of my spiritual freedom in Christ has been the most significant moment of my life.

The release that I felt as years of shame and bondage were lifted from me is hard to describe. I really do not know what to say – I feel like a human being again!

My life has been transformed. It truly was like walking from darkness back into light again.

FICM provided the tool which has allowed me to break the sin-repent-cycle. I am full of hope for the future.

I am a new person and everyone has seen the difference.

Even though I work for a church and have done many things for God, my walk had become a laboured trudge. Yet now I feel so at peace.

I have a clear head, praise Jesus – it hadn't been clear for years!

Finding my freedom in Christ has changed my life.

The everyday problems of life that once seemed so insurmountable are now well in perspective and I am able to tackle most of them in a calm and rational way.

It has transformed my life. I now know God always loves me even though sometimes I might stray from the path he has mapped out for me. I know God is always there, and I marvel at the truth about his kindness, his generosity, and his feelings towards me.

When my ex-husband left, I felt like half a person. I didn't think I should be alone and I didn't feel whole. Those feelings have gone. I feel fulfilled in who I am and am happy with my life.

FREEDOM IN CHRIST *Discipleship Series*

BOOK 1

FREE TO BE YOURSELF

ENJOY YOUR TRUE NATURE IN CHRIST

STEVE GOSS

MONARCH
BOOKS

Oxford, UK & Grand Rapids, Michigan, USA

Published by Monarch Books
an imprint of
Lion Hudson IP Ltd
Wilkinson House, Jordan Hill Road
Oxford OX2 8DR, England
Email: monarch@lionhudson.com
www.lionhudson.com/monarch

ISBN: 978-1-85424-857-2 (UK)
ISBN: 978-0-8254-6189-7 (USA)

First edition 2008

Acknowledgments
Unless otherwise stated, Scripture quotations are taken from the Holy Bible, New International Version, © 1973, 1978, 1984 by the International Bible Society. Used by permission of Hodder and Stoughton Ltd. All rights reserved.

A catalogue record for this book is available from the British Library.

This book is dedicated to my loving parents,
Eifion and Nancy Goss.
Nowadays I routinely come across people whose parents
failed to care for them and nurture them as God intended.
That makes me understand all the more the privilege
I had of being brought up in an environment of love,
respect and support. For their sacrificial love,
careful discipline and constant encouragement that
continues to this day, I am deeply grateful.

Contents

A Special Word of Thanks

I have learned just about everything I know about helping people become fruitful disciples from Neil Anderson, author of *The Bondage Breaker*, *Victory Over the Darkness* and many other books. These are now regarded by many Christians as classics, and rightly so.

It has been my immense privilege to spend time with Neil, to sit under his teaching at many conferences, to collaborate with him in writing *The Freedom In Christ Discipleship Course*, and to have the opportunity to put my questions to him while we were 'on the road' together.

One of the first things I did when I sensed that the Lord might be prompting me to write this series was to ask Neil if he minded. After all, the way he has taught these great biblical principles of freedom is so much part of me now that I could not possibly write these books without using his fundamental methodology.

He had every right to say no and, if he had done that, I would have dropped the project there and then. However, he positively encouraged me to get started and even offered to write a foreword.

For that, and for all he has taught to so many over the years, I am indebted to this man of God who continues to travel the world with this life-changing message.

My thanks go too to Tony Collins and Rod Shepherd at Monarch for their help in getting this series off the ground, as well as to the fantastic team at Freedom In Christ Ministries for their constant support and sacrificial service in taking this message to churches around the country.

Foreword

For twenty-five years I believed in God and regularly attended church. If anyone asked me about my beliefs, I told them that I was a Christian. I looked like a Christian and generally acted like one. In Europe and North America if one respected their parents and wanted to be a 'good boy or girl' it was the cultural thing to be and do. It is sobering to look back and realize that I was one of those millions of cultural 'Christians' who don't have an authentic relationship with their Creator and Heavenly Father. If God hadn't intervened in my life I would have become like the rest of those disillusioned by religion and joined the pagan parade now exiting the culturally or politically correct 'church'.

Religion is the curse of this world, and the force behind many of the conflicts plaguing the planet. However, a relationship with God is our only hope. I was the senior warden of an Episcopal (Anglican) Church and working as an aerospace engineer when I was invited to attend a lay institute for evangelism. I didn't know what that was and had I known I probably wouldn't have gone. The priest wanted me to go with him. So I did, and while learning to share my faith I realized I didn't have any. The presenter asked what difference it would make in our religious beliefs if Christ hadn't come in the flesh? I didn't have an answer. I believed in God and that was enough. Wasn't it?

I heard the gospel for the first time, and gladly gave my heart to Christ and was born again. I became a new creation in Christ, but it took me several years to fully understand what that really meant. At first I was really excited about my new-found faith, and at the same time disappointed in myself for playing 'church' all those years. I couldn't help but wonder how many others were going through the same motions and missing the real relationship that God wants us to have with himself.

Two years later I sensed the call of God to go into full time ministry. The past forty years have been an exciting adventure of learning, growing, and discovering how God sets captives free and binds up their broken hearts. My dear friends and colleagues, Steve and Zoë Goss, have been going through the same transformation and now God is using them to accomplish his work in the United Kingdom.

In writing these four discipleship books, Steve has done a masterful work in presenting the core message of Freedom In Christ Ministries. You will learn, as we have, what difference Christ makes in our 'religious beliefs'. Jesus is the One who died for the sin that has separated us from God. Jesus rose from the dead in order that we can have new life in him. His sacrificial life, death and resurrection also disarmed the god of this world (Colossians 2:15). Jesus came to undo the works of Satan (1 John 3:8) who has deceived the world (Revelation 12:9), and has it under his control (1 John 5:19).

The Church is not an institution for religious observances. It is not an organization, it is an organism. The Church is the body of Christ. The membership is made up of born-again believers who are alive and free in Christ. Their names are written in the Lamb's book of life. 'As many as received him, to them he gave the right to become children of God, to those who believe in his name' (John 1:12). You will discover this and much more as you work your way through this series of discipleship books. So welcome to the family of God. You have many spiritual brothers and sisters in Christ who are learning and growing just as you are. "The Holy Spirit is bearing witness with your spirit that you are a child of God" (Romans 8:16). Have you ever considered what an incredible privilege it is to be called a child of God? The grace of God is truly amazing, and may you grow in that grace and become all that your Heavenly Father created you to be.

Dr. Neil T. Anderson
Founder and President Emeritus of Freedom In Christ Ministries

Be Who You Are!

I have a strong aversion to those books that promise you that your life will change and all will be fine if you will just do A, B and C, followed swiftly by D. If that's what you are looking for, this is not the book for you.

It won't tell you to 'pull yourself together' or 'pray better'. If I manage to leave you with the impression that you need to 'try harder' or anything along those lines, I will have failed.

It is, however, a book for anyone who wants to fulfil all the potential that God has given them – especially, perhaps, those who are tempted to greet that statement with a hollow laugh.

All I want to do is take you back to the moment you made a decision to become a Christian and explain why that was the defining moment of your life.

You already know that, of course. But, if you are anything like me, no one has ever explained to you just how fundamental it was – not only in terms of eternity but for the way you live your life today. Nothing could make more of a difference to the nitty-gritty parts of life: revising for exams; lying in bed with the flu; struggling to cope with a demanding job; talking to your neighbour over the fence.

Just pause for a minute and ask yourself a question. Answer it honestly – try not to be too easy or too hard on yourself. Ready? Here goes... Can you ever really be everything that God wants you to be?

Well, you can probably guess from the title of this book what my response to this question is: yes you can! But bear with me. The worst thing I could do is whip you up into some kind of emotional frenzy where you commit to some kind of false belief that denies reality. No, that's not what I want to do at all.

The fact is that, all through the Bible, it is clear that God is expecting our lives to have good outcomes that please him. He tells us that if we remain in him we will bear much fruit (John 15:5). He tells us to be perfect just as he is (Matthew 5:48) and that we can do everything through him (Philippians 4:13).

Now, does he mean those things or not? I believe he does. But does he *really* mean them, not just in some kind of 'spiritual' or 'theological' sense but in the sense that the words mean exactly what you would expect them to mean if you interpreted them in the most obvious way? To use an analogy, if I am going shopping and you ask me to get you a bar of chocolate and I say that I will, presumably when I return from the shops you fully expect me to hand you a bar of chocolate that you can unwrap and enjoy. You don't expect me to say, 'Just believe I have given you a bar of chocolate' or 'You don't have a physical bar of chocolate but in the heavenly realms it's yours'. No, you expect me to give you what I promised. Let me put my cards on the table. I believe God acts in just the same way. If he says you can be everything he calls you to be, then you can.

The God who loved us so much that he sent his own Son Jesus to die for us is not the sort of God who would say to us, 'Here's a hurdle for you to jump. Go on, jump it', while at the same time knowing full well that it's too high and we cannot do it but will fall flat on our faces. No, if God tells us we can be something or do something, then surely we can – by definition.

I don't know you but I am absolutely certain that *nothing* can stop you becoming a fruitful disciple who gives glory to God and lives for his purposes above everything else. Because that is what God says, and he is God! Is that what you want – to be a fruitful disciple who brings glory to him?

Where we struggle with this, it's not so much to do with

our understanding of what God is saying but with what our own past experiences and feelings have taught us.

Put your feelings to one side for a minute and humour me. What I am going to share with you is not remotely new. I simply want to show how what Jesus accomplished two thousand years ago set in train a chain of events whose logical outcome is so mind-blowing, so radical, that it's difficult to believe. Many don't. The outcome is this: that absolutely nothing and nobody can stop you becoming the person God wants you to be. No circumstance is so difficult, no past event so terrible, no person so powerful that they can stop you fulfilling everything that God has for you.

This is not something for the select few. It's for every Christian (and indeed for those who are not yet Christians). It's especially for those who have 'tried everything', those who feel somewhat weary or disillusioned, those who have experienced difficult circumstances or those who made a commitment to Jesus at one time but now wonder whether they are really Christians at all.

Although it may sound as if this book is about you, in fact it's really about *Jesus Christ* – what he has done, who he is, his astonishing resources, his Kingdom purposes and the exciting place he has called you to occupy in them. It's about knowing him for the wonderful person he is so that we can simply fall at his feet and offer him ourselves completely and utterly.

A time is coming when there is going to be a feast the like of which has never been experienced before. The trumpets will sound and the Bridegroom, Jesus, will come for his bride, the church. She will have made herself ready for him and will be dressed in fine linen. There will be a wedding feast and a new age will be ushered in. You are going to be there.

This book is about helping you to prepare for that moment and bring glory to him. Will the real you please stand up!

Who You Were Meant to Be

In understanding why we are as we are, it's important to recognize that neither we nor the world we grew up in are as God intended. In fact both are quite different.

I recently saw a television series in which people traced their family tree and uncovered something of the lives of their ancestors. It seems that you don't have to go very far back to discover that every family has its fair share of success, shame and secrets. I have spent a little time on my own family tree. I did not know I had any Christian heritage at all, but was surprised and delighted to discover that on both my mother's and my father's side of my family, I had a great-grandfather involved in the Welsh Revival of the 1900s. One of them was known for playing the organ and writing hymns; the other was a preacher. If the musical anointing ever made its way down the family line, it certainly missed me out! On the other hand, I do get to preach from time to time and I love it. It's fascinating to wonder whether something of my great-grandfather's gifting passed down the family line to me. In the television series, people became very emotional as they found out about their ancestors, as if this additional knowledge somehow helped them understand themselves a little better.

I am sure that finding out about our immediate preceding generations does help us understand ourselves to some extent. But if we really want to understand why we are as we are and why we have the inbuilt drives that we do, we need to go a lot further back than that and start with the couple we are all descended from – Adam and Eve.

I was fascinated to discover recently that analysis of

mitochondrial DNA has led scientists to conclude that all human beings are descended from one woman (even if they don't accept that she was necessarily the only one alive at the time), and analysis of Y-chromosomes has led them to the conclusion that all human beings are also descended from one man. I do not pretend to understand this, but it is good to know that the biological evidence is consistent with what the Bible says, because it is all too easy to see the account of Adam and Eve as a kind of fairy story. In fact, the Bible is clear that they were a real couple who lived in a real place (probably somewhere in modern Iraq) at a real time in history.

In trying to understand who we are and what drives us, it's helpful to look at their life just after they were created, because it shows us exactly how God designed us to live and to function. That design has not changed – but, as we shall see, other things have. In Genesis 1:26–28 we read this:

Then God said, 'Let us make man in our image, in our likeness, and let them rule over the fish of the sea and the birds of the air, over the livestock, over all the earth, and over all the creatures that move along the ground.'

So God created man in his own image, in the image of God he created him; male and female he created them. God blessed them and said to them, 'Be fruitful and increase in number; fill the earth and subdue it. Rule over the fish of the sea and the birds of the air and over every living creature that moves on the ground.'

In those three verses, we read three times that men and women were created 'in God's image'. The fish of the sea, the birds of the air and the living creatures that Adam and Eve were to rule over were not created in God's image. To be made in the image of the Creator is an astonishing statement – what does it tell us about who we are or who we were meant to be?

To answer that question, we need to know something of

what God himself is like. Jesus gave us a clue to this when he was talking to a Samaritan woman. He said to her, 'The true worshippers will worship the Father in spirit and truth, for they are the kind of worshippers the Father seeks. God is spirit, and his worshippers must worship in spirit and in truth' (John 4:23–24).

God is spirit. Perhaps the most fundamental way we can answer the question 'What is God like?' is simply to say that God is spirit. Being created in God's image means that fundamentally we too are spirit. Yet, if we are honest, most of us do not think of ourselves primarily as spiritual beings when we consider our identity. For example, if we were to meet at a party and I asked you who you were, what would you say? You would probably give me your name and that would be a reasonable response – but it would tell me very little about who you *are*. Maybe you would go on to talk about your job, your family background or your likes and dislikes. Interesting though those things may be, they do not get to the heart of your identity – who you are deep down inside. In fact, fundamentally, you, like the God in whose image you were made, are spirit. It is not what I can see on the outside that makes up 'the real you' but what is deep inside. We all have both outer and inner persons.

The Bible uses two words, usually translated 'spirit' and 'soul', to refer to our inner person. Theologians have debated for centuries the exact relationship between them. Some say that the spirit and the soul are essentially the same thing. Others think that the word 'soul' refers to our capacity to think, feel and choose, whereas 'spirit' refers to the part of us that lives forever. We probably won't resolve that particular debate this side of heaven, but the key point to note is that we have both an outer person (our body) and an inner person (our soul/spirit). It is not our outer person that is created in the image of God, it's our inner person. It's not our outer person that defines who we are, it's our inner person.

Like us, Adam and Eve were created with both inner and outer persons, and these inner and outer persons were connected. In fact, a good definition of what it means to be physically alive is that your inner person (your soul/spirit) is connected to your outer person (your physical body).

But Adam and Eve were not just physically alive. They were also spiritually alive. That is different and means that their inner person (their soul/spirit) was connected to God. That is how we were designed to be too: on the one hand, our spirit connected to our physical body (physically alive); and on the other hand, our spirit connected to God (spiritually alive).

If Adam died physically, his spirit would separate from his body but he would still be connected to God. As Paul put it, he would be 'away from the body and at home with the Lord' (2 Corinthians 5:8). He may not have his body any longer, but he would still intrinsically be Adam.

Deep down inside we are spiritual beings. Why not pause and think for a moment to let that sink in... Does it feel like you have an inner person quite apart from your body? Where does your appreciation of music or sunsets come from?

In fact, the Bible assures us that at every level of life the ultimate reality in the universe is spiritual, not physical. Every physical thing we see is only temporary and will pass away, but spiritual things last for ever (2 Corinthians 4:18). The invisible world is just as real as the visible world (Hebrews 11:3). So our fundamental identity – who we really are – comes from our inner spiritual person, not from our outer physical person. The part of us that, more than anything else, defines who we really are cannot be put under a microscope and examined but is just as real as those parts of us that can. If anything, it is more important than our body. One day our body will die and we will leave it behind but our spirit will go on forever.

Spiritual life is where it's at

It was this fundamental spiritual connection to God that made Adam's life so very different from the one we were born with. Being spiritually alive gave him a whole different quality of life from mere physical existence.

In July 1967 the BBC broadcast its first TV programme in colour, a four-hour live broadcast from the Wimbledon Tennis Championship. I lived in one of the areas whose transmitters carried those early colour broadcasts, and our next-door neighbour bought a colour TV. I remember (only just, you understand!) going into their lounge with a whole crowd of people from our street to watch it. To be honest, the quality was not that great but, when you were used to plain black-and-white pictures, seeing colour pictures was nothing short of astonishing. When we only had the possibility of black-and-white pictures, they seemed fine because that was our only expectation. But seeing colour pictures opened up a whole new world, and black-and-white could never be the same again.

The difference between mere physical existence and abundant spiritual life is something like that. When you don't know anything but physical life, you don't know what you're missing. But taste life as it was meant to be in its glorious spiritual abundance, and a mere physical existence seems decidedly monochrome. As we shall see, however, it's possible to have the gift of spiritual life but not realize what it means or just how amazing it is.

So what did it mean for Adam and Eve to be spiritually alive? What were the key differences between spiritual life and a mere physical existence?

Significance

Being spiritually alive meant that Adam had an innate sense of significance. As we have seen, God gave him an amazing purpose for his life: to rule over the world (Genesis 1:26). You don't get much more significant than that!

I don't know about you, but as far back as I can remember, I have been aware of thinking, 'There must be more to life', of looking for some deeper meaning. In effect I was trying to understand my own significance. That is in stark contrast to my two dogs who have only physical life and were made just for physical life. As long as they can eat, sleep, go for walks and sniff other dogs, they are perfectly happy. That is just not enough for me!

Adam simply would not have had that nagging feeling that there must be more. He had no need to search for significance or meaning in life – he simply had it. It was just part of the way God had made him.

Security

There was another crucial thing that being spiritually alive gave Adam. He felt totally safe and secure in God's presence. In fact, it wasn't just a feeling, it was an ever-present reality. Everything he needed was provided – food, shelter, companionship – everything.

There was no need to worry about health or finance or what others thought. In fact, he would have had no concept of what it was to go without. I don't know what language Adam and Eve spoke, but I am pretty sure it had no word for 'need'.

Acceptance

Adam also had a relationship with God that was astonishingly intimate. He could talk with him at any time and have his full attention. God would speak back to him tenderly, clearly, lovingly... Imagine that!

Then God created Eve for Adam – and she was a perfect companion (Genesis 1:27–28). They complemented each other superbly. They were accepted by God and each other. They were naked yet unashamed – nothing to hide, nothing to cover up. They had an intimate relationship with each other in the presence of God. Both of them had an amazing sense of belonging, not just to God but to another human being.

Stop and think for a minute what their life was like. At our conferences I often ask people to consider what Adam and Eve would have thought about as they dropped off to sleep each night. After all, they would have had absolutely nothing to worry about – no mortgage to pay off; no difficult colleagues or family; no health worries. The more 'spiritual' attendees tend to say that they would have been thinking about God and his goodness. Others are of the view that they were probably thinking about each other!

These were real people at a real time – not some abstract theological concept. They did not float ethereally around the garden – they had real work to do. They would have had the deepest experiences of companionship and intimacy; they would have had such fun. The end of each day would have brought the deepest sense of satisfaction.

Their world was so different from our own. But *that world* is the one that you were designed to live in. The spiritual life that came from the connection to God truly was abundant, amazing, exhilarating. That life, with its total security, real purpose, no worries, and intimate, satisfying relationships, was the life that you were designed to live.

The world they lived in was totally different from the one we were born into. The life they had bore little resemblance to our early experiences on earth. Yet our entire beings were made for that world and that life – not the one we ended up with.

Who You Were When You Were Born

The consequences of the Fall

Adam and Eve were free to do just about anything. They could eat from any of the trees in the garden – and there must have been thousands – except one. That one tree probably held no great interest for them until Satan drew their attention to it and tempted them to doubt God and his trustworthiness and love.

At that time, Satan had to crawl at their feet like a snake. He could not harm them in any way. He had no way of forcing them to do what he wanted. All he could do was tempt them and deceive them. But they fell for it. Satan offered them something more than the abundance God had given them. He implied that God was not being straight with them. They believed him and went ahead and ate from the tree. Disobeying God is what the Bible calls 'sin'.

Look at the exact words God had said to them: 'You must not eat from the tree of the knowledge of good and evil, for when you eat of it you will surely die' (Genesis 2:17). Well, they did eat. Did they die? They certainly did not die physically – at least not for 900 years or so (which was a pretty good innings, if you ask me). So how did they die? Spiritually. In other words, the connection that their spirits had to God was broken. They were still physically alive so could still function on a physical level (just like my dogs), but they were separated from God and from his abundant life.

We will go on to look at some of the specific consequences

of their sin, which are many and varied. However, they can all be summed up in just one word: death.

Up to now this story may have seemed somewhat removed from us. It may not even appear to have any relevance at all to our daily lives. But here's the rub. Because they sinned and lost that crucial spiritual connection to God, all of their descendants were born without it too. According to Paul, you (and everyone else) 'were dead in your transgressions and sins' (Ephesians 2:1). Clearly you were not physically dead – you were able to function physically – but there was no connection to God. You were spiritually dead.

Sometimes the account of Adam and Eve in the garden seems like something of a fairy story. It's so removed from our experience. Actually, it's something of a horror story. I don't know that we are capable of imagining the absolute horror and terror they must have felt after they had sinned. The contrast between the final day that Adam and Eve were spiritually alive and the next day when they were not was stark, as we shall see. For us, however, born without that spiritual life and not having known any different, it's not so easy to recognize what is going on inside.

When Adam and Eve sinned (something often described as 'the Fall') and were banished from God's presence, they lost the intimate knowledge of God they had once enjoyed. Being spiritually dead meant that the intimate relationship they had had with God came to an abrupt end. It must have been devastating suddenly to lose that. No longer could they speak to God and depend on his wisdom. No longer could they call out to him and simply bask in his glorious presence.

That meant that they had to work things out on their own without being able to rely on God's wisdom. They had to work out key issues such as their identity, purpose and meaning in life independently of God. They didn't have a clue how to do it. They had no idea how to behave – a fact that became abundantly clear when Adam tried to hide from a God who knows everything and is everywhere (Genesis 3:7–8)!

Paul described Adam's descendants like this: 'They are darkened in their understanding and separated from the life of God because of the ignorance that is in them due to the hardening of their hearts' (Ephesians 4:18). They are darkened in their understanding because they no longer have that connection to God because, as he puts it, they are 'separated from the life of God'. Note again that it is this spiritual life (the life of God who is spirit) that is key. Paul reinforces this elsewhere when he tells us that a natural person (i.e. one who is spiritually dead) simply cannot discern the things of God because they have to be discerned spiritually (1 Corinthians 2:14).

That's how we came into the world: without a true knowledge of God. We may have come to know about God, but we can't really know him until we establish a real relationship with him through Jesus Christ (1 Corinthians 2:14). Really knowing God is about an intimate relationship – not just knowing facts about him. You hear about people who meet over the internet, exchange e-mails and then get married. But what kind of marriage would you have if you continued to communicate by e-mail, perhaps sending the occasional digital photo? Certainly not a very intimate one!

Feeling bad

Can you imagine how Adam and Eve must have felt the day after they sinned? The sky and the rivers probably looked the same, but in fact nothing was the same. It must have been the worst 'morning after' feeling ever.

They had foolishly thrown away their positions of security, significance and acceptance, and were the first to understand the truth of the saying that you don't miss it until it's gone.

What they then immediately began to experience was the very opposite of the position they had so recently held. They were overwhelmed by a whole series of negative emotions that they had never known before. Those negative emotions stayed with them for the rest of their lives and are also the lot of their descendants.

Instead of knowing absolute unassailable security, they were now overwhelmed by fear and anxiety. In fact, the very first recorded emotion was expressed by Adam: 'I was afraid' (Genesis 3:10). Interestingly, 'Do not be afraid' is the most repeated commandment in the Bible. Today, anxiety disorders are the number-one mental health problem in the world.

This is not how it was meant to be. Things had been turned on their head. People who had been lovingly created to know nothing but security suddenly experienced the opposite. How they must have longed to return to where they were just twenty-four hours previously – but they could not.

At least Adam and Eve understood why they had that deep need within them to return to the position of security they had lost. We, however, were born with that same deep need but without the same understanding. We did not know that we were only ever meant to know absolute security in the hands of a loving, unassailable God. All we knew is that we often felt anxious or afraid.

Adam's fall from grace created in his descendants a need at the deepest level to get back to the position that Adam originally had. It's just that until we come to Christ, none of us realizes where it comes from or what to do about it.

Originally, they had a sense of significance. When the relationship with God was broken, again they suddenly experienced the opposite. They felt insignificant and had a sense of guilt and shame. The world around them must suddenly have seemed a strange and forbidding place.

What had originally been a very good thing for Adam and Eve became a glaring need in us: we are all born wanting to get back to the sense of significance that Adam and Eve had originally. We hear a lot today about lack of self-esteem, and negative self-image. They have been problems ever since the Fall.

Originally, they had a sense of belonging, of complete acceptance. When the relationship with God was broken, there came a crushing sense of rejection. Everyone is born with it and it creates in us a driving need to be accepted. That's why it takes great courage to stand alone against what others say or think. Our need to belong, to fit in, to be accepted by others, is so strong.

Originally, Adam and Eve had God's power within them. Nothing could stop them being everything God wanted them to be and doing everything God called them to do. That all changed completely. Now they had to rely on their own strength and resources.

What about you? Well, you came into the world and you were designed to be secure, significant and accepted. But it gradually dawned on you as you grew up that you were not secure, significant and accepted – or at least that not everyone thought you were!

That's why, from an early age, we grow up trying to exercise some control over our lives. To some degree or other, we have all felt alone in a world that we cannot control. We were not designed, of course, to be in control. We were made to be completely dependent on God, but we didn't know that – and more importantly, we didn't know him – so we had no choice but to try to control our own destinies.

Some of us are more able than others to do that, but ultimately none of us can control our environment completely. Even the richest and most powerful people in the world cannot keep going for ever – all of them ultimately succumb to things they cannot control, whether it's a war or a health issue.

The American multi-millionaire Malcolm Forbes was one of the super rich. He owned eight homes including a palace in Morocco, a chateau in France and an island in Fiji. He accumulated 2,200 paintings and twelve Russian Imperial Fabergé eggs. In a TV interview he said, 'All I want to do is live long enough to enjoy all that I have.' Asked if he believed in life after death, he answered, 'Life after death will be no comparison to the life I am now living. I have the best possible life right now. It could never be any better.' A few months later, Forbes died. All his wealth could do nothing to prevent his death. Furthermore, it offered him no protection whatsoever when he then had to stand before God.

I have met several people – both female and male – who suffer from anorexia, and I have seen some find their freedom in Christ and walk away from it. It's a dreadful illness and in the worst cases, sufferers slowly kill themselves. The media tell us that this illness is all to do with people's desire to be slim and attractive. Certainly self-image is part of the problem but, in my experience, that is not the main issue. It seems in fact to be a kind of coping mechanism that people have developed to deal with feelings of being out of control. Jane, for example, was a pastor's wife who ate normally most of the time. However, at times of stress when she didn't seem to be able to control her world, she would stop eating. It's as if she had concluded that there was no way that she could control the world 'out there', so instead she would blot it out by concentrating on something that was under her control – her intake of food. Sufferers get a sense of satisfaction from exercising that control. They are able to avoid deeper issues by using all their energies to control their own bodies. Freedom comes when they are able to hand over that sense of being out of control to God and trust him with the outcome, much as Adam and Eve did instinctively before the Fall.

I run a small mail order business with half my time. That's where I tend to learn most of my faith lessons. I have noticed in my business life that when things are tough financially, I have a tendency to ignore the major issues (because they seem to be out of my control) and concentrate on things that are trivial but absorbing. Instead of addressing the fact that I need to work out how to pay a large supplier who might cut off my credit if I don't do something soon, I might spend a day buried in a trivial computer problem. When I do that, I am simply engaging in the same kind of behaviour that anorexics display.

Perhaps the saddest people are those who try to control their world through controlling other people, manipulating them to do or say the right things. It may work for a time but it never works for long. Someone with a tendency to try to control others is likely to be just about the most insecure person you could ever meet.

We can surmise, considering everything we've just looked at, that Adam and Eve would also have felt depressed and angry. How could they not? Again we find that our experience mirrors this. A study done a few years ago in the UK found that 25 per cent of women and 10 per cent of men will have at least one clinical episode of depression before they are 65. (How come, incidentally, our ladies are more depressed than our men? Perhaps it's something to do with the people they live with!)

In fact, if you could really get your mind around how it was meant to be and how it is now, you would probably feel pretty depressed and angry too, even if you simply consider the effects of Adam's sin on your life. The consequences are so huge that it's almost impossible to take them in.

How You Tried to Be You

A few years ago my wife Zoë and I travelled with some friends to the Lake District for New Year. I drove us up there in a brand-new company car – big, red and shiny. It was my first 'executive' model and I was proud of it. On New Year's Day the weather was glorious, so what could be better than to go for a morning drive in the breathtaking scenery? We headed for a narrow road that led up the side of a mountain to an area where there were spectacular views. At a certain point on the road, we came to a large handwritten sign that someone had propped up at the side of the road. It read 'Danger – ice. Turn round.' Well, the road ahead looked fine and the sun was shining, so I simply ignored it. We began climbing steeply, the narrow road clinging to the side of the mountain with an increasingly steep drop on one side. I suddenly became aware of the engine revving much more loudly than usual. It took one of my friends to tell me that this meant that the wheels were spinning on black ice. There was absolutely no possibility at that point of stopping to turn round – the road simply was not wide enough. So we had to keep heading upwards, wheels spinning, perilously close to the edge, making slow progress until we finally reached a point where we could turn round. That wasn't the end of the story because we then had to drive down the same steep, icy road with the perilous drop, hoping that we would not simply skid off the edge. To make matters worse, we encountered others on their way up, wheels spinning madly. We had to inch past each other so close to the edge that the void was all we could see from one side of the car. We finally got back to the sign about forty-five minutes and a lifetime later.

Like Adam and Eve's journey to the point where they were deceived, our outward journey seemed fine. But it didn't end up where we thought it would. And the big question was, how on earth were we going to get back?

That's the question Adam and Eve faced the morning after and for the rest of their lives: was it possible to go back? There did not seem any way back for them. It's also the question that all of us face practically from the moment we are born, even though we do not understand our circumstances sufficiently to articulate it. From our earliest moments we set about trying to find the way back to life as God intended it to be, the life that he created us to live. We don't understand it but we desperately want to go back to where Adam and Eve were. Because that's how we were created to be.

We may not understand why we have those deep, urgent needs for significance, security and acceptance, and we almost certainly cannot articulate those feelings deep within, but instinctively we are trying to meet those needs.

There is nothing wrong in that, incidentally. God created us to have security, significance and acceptance in him. We are created to have those things. It's perfectly OK for us to want to feel secure, to know that we are significant and to feel that we are unconditionally accepted for who we are.

But is it possible to go back to the position Adam and Eve had before the Fall? Or do we have no option but to stay up the mountain, wheels spinning, or even worse, plunge off the edge?

The world's false promises

As we grew up and were instinctively searching for that way back, the world told us that it could take us there. In fact, it continues to make bold promises that it is the way back, that it can fulfil our deepest needs.

It says that if you get some good qualifications under your belt or you become an outstanding sportsperson...if you can successfully keep all the plates spinning...if you can do all the things people expect and more...then you will be significant.

If you want to be secure, says the world, get some money behind you. Get a good salary and a big house. Or simply flaunt the symbols of worldly success – designer clothes, flashy cars – and people will assume you have the money that goes with them and give you honour and respect. That will make you feel secure.

Do you want to be accepted by others? Well, says the world, get people to like you. You simply have to look fantastic – and there are any number of routes to that from high fashion to liposuction. You need to make others admire you, or even desire you. If you want intimacy, the world says it can be found in the act of sex. Many buy that lie and sleep around because they desperately want to be accepted and have the intimate relationship they were created to have.

Again, let's remember that it is not wrong to want to be significant, secure and accepted. You were made for that. Ultimately, however, the best the world can offer does not work because it all depends on what we *do*. It comes down to our own efforts. Yet every single one of us wants, deep down, to be loved unconditionally for who we *are*, not because of what we *do*. Appearance, performance, and social status can never recapture what Adam and Eve lost.

Let's note in passing, however, that the world's promises do work to some extent – at least for a while. We do feel significant when we perform well, secure when we have money in the bank and more coming in, and accepted when others admire us. But those feelings do not – indeed cannot – last. None of us can outperform others all of the time; it only takes a stock-market crash or a terrorist outrage to make us realize that our money really does not buy security; and none of us can keep our good looks for ever.

It's often those who have had the best the world can offer who are the first to realize that its promises are ultimately empty. Consider the example of Solomon in the Old Testament, who was King of Israel at its greatest time. He had the position and power to do whatever he wanted to do, and he had the wealth to finance it – we still hear of King Solomon's mines. He had all the women any man could want and more. At one time he probably believed that the world could deliver on its promises. But when he tried the things it was offering, he realized that he was trying to find purpose and meaning in life independently of God, and that it didn't work. He had the benefit, of course, of the fact that God gave him more wisdom than anyone else, so he was able to make a wise judgment about what he discovered. He wrote a book about his conclusions in the Old Testament entitled Ecclesiastes. And what did he conclude? 'Utterly meaningless! Everything is meaningless' (Ecclesiastes 1:2).

Bernhard Langer, a top golfer who is also a Christian, came to the same conclusion:

> By the time I was about 28 years old, I had basically achieved almost everything that I wanted to. I realized that material things don't make you happy and that there must be more in this life than just accumulating money in the bank, or cars, or houses, or whatever. You just want more, more, more and are never satisfied.

The great majority of people, however, never get to the point where they feel they have 'enough' of what the world promises and they spend their whole life trying to get there. Of course, everyone agrees that money cannot buy us happiness – at least on one level – but it's amazing how many who say that actually live their lives as if it does.

We can't get back the life that Adam had by trying harder or by dressing to impress, because the problem is that we were born separated from God, without the life of God within us.

Religion's false promises

Getting back into a right relationship with God is a much more promising way of trying to get back to the position we were always meant to have. The big question is, how can that be done?

People throughout the centuries in all major religions have realized that we need to please God, to become acceptable to him. So far, so good. But then they have concluded that that means living up to certain standards, obeying a set of rules.

However, in the Old Testament, God demonstrated clearly that that does not work. He made a covenant with humankind based on the concept of Law. It went like this: if we could live according to the Law (a set of rules that he gave us) by human effort, then we would be blessed. If we couldn't, we would be cursed. We couldn't.

The Law was powerless to give us back the life that Adam and Eve lost (Galatians 3:10, 21). In fact, even though in itself the Law is a good thing, the effect of our inability to obey it was that the Law actually functioned as a curse for us. Paul explains that God always intended the Law to be a kind of teacher – it was designed to teach us our need of Christ (Galatians 3:24). He had to make us aware of the utter hopelessness of our position, a hopelessness caused by spiritual death – that is to say, separation from God.

The fact is that people without spiritual life in them are incapable of pleasing God. There is nothing they can do to change that. Religions still peddle the lie, however, that we can please God by our own efforts. Christianity is not exempt from this: it's not at all uncommon to find churches giving the impression that we can earn God's favour – or, more usually, maintain God's favour – by what we do. The truth is, we cannot.

You may think that it is well understood today that obeying rules does not get us back into a right relationship with God. Yet I constantly meet Christians who, although they would go along with that sentiment, in effect live as though they can earn God's favour by how they behave, by what they do or don't do. They have come to believe that pleasing God is something that can be earned by adhering to a particular standard.

The trouble with this approach – which is often called 'legalism' – is that it emphasizes external behaviour rather than internal devotion. God has always made clear that he is interested in our hearts, because what we do will spring from what's going on inside. Legalism is a kind of slap in the face to God because it says that, although God's grace may be able to forgive me of my sin, it cannot make me totally acceptable before God. For that I need to *do* things as well. Those who get caught up in it tend to exhibit characteristics such as drivenness, independence and judging others. God's heart is for people to choose to do what is right simply out of love for him, not because they are looking for acceptance or feel that they somehow have to.

In many ways the false promises of the world and the false promises of religion are based on the same big lie: that we can *do* something to get back to the position we were designed to have. In fact, there is not a thing we can *do*. Left to ourselves, there simply is no way back. We are in a hopeless position.

Who You Are Now

The only possible answer to our predicament is somehow to restore our relationship with God, to reconnect our spirit to God's Spirit, to become spiritually alive again. That was not something we could accomplish ourselves. It is something where God had to take the initiative. Thankfully, he is a God of mercy and grace, and he found a way. He sent Jesus.

If I were to ask you why Jesus came, what would your response be? Actually, I've tried this question many times and most Christians will say something along the lines of, 'He came to forgive our sins.' That is true. But if we think that was the main objective of Jesus' coming, we may have missed the point. Let's see what Jesus himself had to say:

> *'I have come that they may have life, and have it to the full.'*
> (JOHN 10:10)

There's that word 'life' again. What was it that Adam lost? Life! What did Jesus come to give us? Life! In fact, once you get that kind of orientation, you see that word 'life' all over the New Testament, and in the most significant places:

> *In the beginning was the Word... In him was life, and that life was the light of men.* (JOHN 1:1-4)

It's interesting to note here that the *life* was the light of men – the life came before the light. Fundamentally, it's this spiritual life that is the real issue.

'I am the resurrection and the life. *He who believes in me will* live, *even though he dies.'*   (JOHN 11:25)

In other words, he will live *spiritually*, even if he dies *physically*.

Jesus was like Adam in that he was both physically and spiritually alive. His spiritual life came from the fact that God himself was his actual biological Father. Like Adam, Jesus was tempted by Satan. Unlike Adam, however, Jesus never sinned.

He went willingly to the cross, suffering unimaginable torment. He did indeed die for our sin, taking the penalty due to us in his own body – but it was a means to an end. The whole point of that was so that he could make a way for us to get back the spiritual life we were designed to have.

That spiritual life is often referred to as 'eternal life'. At one time I thought it was what Christians get when they die. In fact, it's even better than that – it's a whole different quality of life *right now* as well as something that will indeed last for ever. It's what makes the difference as we face life's daily challenges and struggles. In fact, it's simply getting back the spiritual life that Adam lost at the Fall.

The Lord in his wisdom has given me a reminder of that in the shape of my lovely and long-suffering wife. Her parents gave her the name Zoë – they may have known that it meant 'life' but at that time they were not active Christians and I suspect they just liked the sound of it. There are two Greek words used for 'life' in the New Testament. The first is *bios*, which simply means physical life and is the root of our word 'biology'. But *zoe* is spiritual life, life of a completely different order. This is how C. S. Lewis sums it up in *Mere Christianity*:

> *The Biological sort which comes to us through Nature, and which (like everything else in Nature) is always tending to run down and decay so that it can only be kept up by incessant subsidies from Nature in the form of air, water, food, etc., is*

> *Bios. The Spiritual life which is in God from all eternity, and which made the whole natural universe, is Zoe. Bios has, to be sure, a certain shadowy or symbolic resemblance to Zoe: but only the sort of resemblance there is between a photo and a place, or a statue and a man. A man who changed from having Bios to having Zoe would have gone through as big a change as a statue which changed from being a carved stone to being a real man.* (PP. 139–140, MACMILLAN PAPERBACKS EDITION)

Or, as I said earlier, it's a bit like the difference between colour and black-and-white television.

Spiritual life restores our significance, security and acceptance

In 1 John 5:12, John wrote, 'He who has the Son has life; he who does not have the Son does not have life.' You either have it or you don't. But, if you have made a decision to make Jesus Lord of your life, then you have that spiritual life right now – although it may not feel like it. When we become Christians our spirit is reconnected to God's Spirit – we are spiritually born again, and we can know God and relate to others in the same intimate way that Adam and Eve knew.

As we have already noted, getting that spiritual life back is what we have been working for all our lives – even if we have not realized it. Along with that reconnection to God, we get back everything that comes with being spiritually alive, specifically the *significance*, *security* and *acceptance* that were always meant to be ours.

At a stroke this resolves the struggle that we have had all of our life to work out who we are, and the deep need we have had to be accepted, secure, and significant. If you are a Christian, you are right now just as significant, secure and accepted as Adam was before he sinned.

This is a difficult one to get our minds around, isn't it? That's because we have spent the whole of our lives looking for those things somewhere else, and it doesn't *feel* as if they are met in Christ. This is where we come to a question that we will return to time and again: are you going to believe what your feelings (based on your past experiences) tell you, or are you going to believe what God tells you in his Word? Assuming you are prepared to make the choice to believe what God says in his Word, despite your feelings and circumstances, let's look at what he has to say to those who are in Christ about our deepest needs for significance, security and acceptance.

You are significant

We may have come to believe through past experiences or what others have said to us that we are worthless, inadequate or hopeless. The Bible, however, assures us that that is absolutely not the case. You can say with boldness, 'I am significant'!

One of my favourite verses is Ephesians 2:10 which says that we are, each one of us, 'God's workmanship'. The Greek word used means a work of art. You are so precious to God that you are like a great work of art that he is creating lovingly and painstakingly. I like to think of God as a sculptor carefully chiselling away at my life so that something beautiful gradually emerges from a featureless block of stone. Perhaps you might prefer to think of yourself as a breathtaking painting appearing on a canvas or a beautiful poem or a complex novel.

The same verse tells us that God has prepared in advance some specific 'good works' for us to do. Those things will be different for you than for me. How amazing to think that the Creator of the world has planned some things specifically for you to do. He knows you so well and has taken pains to ensure that they are exactly right for you. How much more significant could you possibly get than that!

But there's more, much more. How about 1 Corinthians 3:16–17 which says, 'Don't you know that you yourselves are God's temple and that God's Spirit lives in you? If anyone destroys God's temple, God will destroy him; for God's temple is sacred, and you are that temple.'

The picture of the Temple that Paul uses here was particularly meaningful for its original audience. They understood just how holy the Temple was. It was the place where God lived on earth. Only one person – the High Priest – was allowed to go into the most holy place and then only once a year (see Hebrews 9:7). When he was there, he had to sprinkle blood as a sin offering for himself and the people. What an enormous contrast to your position right now. The High Priest simply had the privilege of going into the most holy place, not without some fear and trepidation and only once a year. You actually *are* the most holy place! God, the most high God, the God who is 'holy, holy, holy', has chosen to live in you!

You don't any longer have to cower in fear before God as the High Priest had to. In Christ you can approach him 'with freedom and confidence' (Ephesians 3:12).

Still not convinced about your astonishing significance? Try pondering this fact. If you had been the only person in the whole world who had needed Jesus to die for them, he would have done it just for you. That is how significant you are.

You are secure

Eternal security

I recall eavesdropping on a conversation my younger daughter was having with her friend who had come to sleep over when they were aged around seven. Her friend was from a family of Jehovah's Witnesses and they got to talking about what happens to you when you die. I'm not sure whether she was reflecting actual Jehovah's Witnesses' beliefs or not, but the friend was very clear. She said that first of all, all the Jehovah's Witnesses get to go to heaven and then everyone else does as well. My daughter, however, equally clearly, said, 'No, Christians go to heaven and everyone else goes to hell.' There was silence for a while and then my daughter spoke again: 'You know what... If you're right, I'm OK. But if I'm right, you're in big trouble!' And that's the truth. If we are not accepted by God, then we really are in trouble.

The whole thrust of the New Testament is to give us a wonderful assurance that in Christ we are no longer guilty, unprotected, alone or abandoned but are absolutely and totally secure. In just one chapter of Romans, God assures you that you are free forever from any condemnation (Romans 8:1–2), that he is making sure that all things are working together for your good (verse 28) and that you cannot be separated from the love of God (verses 35–39). You can't get more secure than that!

Yet I come across many Christians who feel insecure and doubt that they are really saved. It's an area where Satan will attack if he can. For most of us it takes the form of a niggling doubt that robs us of our joy. Sometimes, however, it becomes more obvious that Satan is involved. Here's an extreme example taken from an e-mail sent to me:

I received Christ with an open longing heart, and He met me. I was so grateful and happy. Three weeks after my conversion I heard a voice ask a question,

'I wonder if it's possible to do something against God now you are a child of God?'

My first reaction was, 'I do not want to do any thing against God. I love Him.'

'But, wouldn't it be great to FEEL the power of God keeping you from doing this against Him?'

'Well, the only thing I know to do against God would be to blaspheme the Holy Spirit. But I would be horrified to do that.'

'You could try! You could FEEL God's power and presence when He keeps you from doing it, and if He doesn't stop you He will know you did not mean what you said, so He will forgive you.'

I did it (foolish me!!!). I spoke the words but I did not mean any of them. I just tried to see if I could say it. God did not stop me. Immediately after I had said it, the voice said, 'Now you have done it! God hates you! You are doomed to hell!'

I cried for forgiveness, but I could not believe God would forgive me. Thoughts of blasphemies were shot into my head like an automatic gun with all sorts of blasphemies against the Holy Trinity. At the same time a wind of fear, anguish and condemnation swept into my emotions.

For three years I lived with this constant torment day and night. My grades in school dropped and I was thinking of suicide. Then one day when I was on my way to church for the second time that day I heard a voice again say: 'Give up! Say out loud that you curse God, Jesus and the Holy Spirit! God already hates you and has not forgiven you and your Christian life doesn't work. God does not help you. He has abandoned you. Say it out loud!'

I thought NO! NO! NO! NEVER! The anguish got worse and worse, and I felt I could not resist. I could not stand the anguish. I was also frustrated because I had cried for help to God so desperately day and night for many years, and I felt that He had not helped me. I was angry too. At last I gave in and said: 'I don't give a **** about this damned thing!' I meant the whole mental disturbance which I had experienced, but when I had said this, the voice said 'Also add that you mean that you curse the Holy Trinity'. And I agreed that I meant the Holy Trinity too. I did not say it, but agreed to mean it. I did not want to do that! I was so frustrated and angry at that time that I agreed, but at the same time my innermost being that was my real me shouted: – NOOOOOOOOOOOOOOO!

Have you ever heard a similar story from someone else? I am starting to believe it must have been demons that were speaking to me, because this was really different from my own normal thinking.

I received Christ. I became His child. But then I turned from God and I am tempted to believe that I am no longer in Christ, so I do not have the right to call myself His child with all that that means. Romans 8:1 is not for me, because I am no longer in Christ. I have thrown myself out of His hand.

If you have anything to say I would be so GRATEFUL!

It may surprise you to hear that I have come across many Christians with similar stories. We'll examine the cause of the 'voice' and how to deal with it in the next book in this series. For now we want to concentrate on the serious question being raised. Had the person lost their salvation because they had given into temptation and 'cursed' the Holy Trinity? This was part of my response:

In our experience there are many Christians who experience the same battle for the mind as you are experiencing. And we know of many Christians who have done the same thing you have done out of desperation.

When you became a Christian you were not just given a gift of eternal life. You became a whole new person. You changed from being someone who could not help but displease God to someone who is now holy, righteous and pleasing to God. This happened because of what Christ did on the cross and has nothing to do with how you behave.

Jesus put it like this (John 10:28–29): 'I give them eternal life, and they shall never perish; no one can snatch them out of my hand. My Father, who has given them to me, is greater than all; no one can snatch them out of my Father's hand.'

If you have made a genuine commitment to Jesus, you are 100% secure in Him. That ongoing security does not depend on your behaviour but on what He has done. If it is a genuine commitment, it will, of course, work out in your behaviour (you will want to do things that please Him) but when you make a mistake as in the case you describe, this is what happens:

Hebrews 4:15–16: 'For we do not have a high priest who is unable to sympathize with our weaknesses, but we have one who has been tempted in every way, just as we are – yet was without sin. Let us then approach the throne of grace with confidence, so that we may receive mercy and find grace to help us in our time of need.'

You have found someone, Jesus, who loves you, sympathizes with your weaknesses and lets you approach Him with confidence so that He can give you mercy and grace.

The very fact that this bothers you so much says to me that your commitment is genuine, that you have passed from death to life, that your salvation is absolutely secure. It is those who do not care who are in effect committing the unforgivable sin – they refuse to turn to Christ to receive their salvation. That is not where you are.

All that is happening is that you are experiencing a battle for your mind. You have an enemy who wants to stop you being fruitful. As long as he is able to convince you that you are not really a Christian or that God has abandoned you, he will be succeeding. You quote Romans 8:1 which says that there is no condemnation for those who are in Christ Jesus. In fact, your head is full of condemning thoughts. The key point, however, is that none of those condemning thoughts is from God. Every one of them originates with the enemy. They are not true.

All the time we believe that our salvation is dependent on our behaviour, we will be insecure. When we finally realize the glorious truth that it is dependent on what Christ has done and that he has made us completely new creations, then we can begin to experience something of the security that Adam and Eve must have felt in the garden, when they had no concept whatsoever of any danger or the possibility of being separated from God.

That is not to say that we should take the matter of sinful behaviour lightly, as if sin is not a serious thing. It is. Falling for Satan's lies and giving in to temptation affect our relationship with God – but not at the level of our eternal security. Until we resolve the sin issue through repentance and resisting the enemy, it will also prevent us from being fruitful and living out our new identity in Christ. We will look at this in more detail in the next books in this series.

Day-to-day security

For most of us, however, this whole question of how secure we feel is less to do with our eternal salvation and more to do with day-to-day life – typically, issues of health and finance.

A lady once came up to me at one of our conferences and showed me a newspaper cutting of her story. It contained a picture of her holding her wheelchair above her head. She related how she had been diagnosed with an incurable muscle-wasting disease but had then been through the Freedom In Christ teaching and The Steps To Freedom In Christ, a structured process of putting things right with God. After going through the Steps, she found she was able to get out of her wheelchair and walk, and has never looked back. Seven or so years on, I understand that she is still fine.

The interesting thing to me, however, is that she said to me, 'But my healing was not the most important thing about the Steps. I also had anorexia and I was able to walk away from that too because I discovered who I am in Christ – knowing that has changed my life.'

I want to contrast that with someone else, also in a wheelchair, who was desperate for me to take him through the Steps To Freedom In Christ because he wanted to be healed of a similar condition. I understand that completely but, as I talked to him about his life and circumstances, I found myself wondering whether healing was actually what the Lord wanted for him at that point. It seemed to me that he wanted to be healed so that he could resume his high-earning career and demonstrate to his father that he was worth something. It looked to me as if he probably needed to re-evaluate his belief system to get it in line with what would really bring him significance and acceptance. He needed to understand that he was already incredibly valuable and didn't need to get back on a treadmill to prove it to anybody. I said that I would take him through the Steps process, but only if he was doing it with the sole objective of getting himself radically right with God. I said that if God chose to heal him too, that should be regarded as a bonus, but there was no guarantee that it would happen. I never heard from him again.

I regularly hear stories of people who have been healed after going through the Steps. I don't pretend to understand how this works. I suspect that sometimes the enemy has been able to get enough influence in their lives that he is able to mimic the symptoms of genuine diseases, and when they resolve spiritual conflicts he is not able to do that any more. On the other hand, I am sure that the Lord sometimes miraculously heals people from genuine diseases, and the gift of healing is one of the gifts that the Holy Spirit distributes among his people.

I do not, however, find in the New Testament grounds to believe that all Christians can expect to be healed physically by God as a matter of course. Unless the Lord returns before, we are all going to die because our physical bodies remain affected by the Fall.

So can we feel secure about our health as Christians? Yes! Even though our physical bodies will fail us, we are eventually going to get an amazing new body that will last for ever. There will be no more suffering, no more sickness. Death, therefore, is not something to be feared for the Christian.

Having seen some of my family and friends die of cancer, however, I confess that I view the process of dying as a somewhat scary prospect. I keep reminding myself of the firm promise Jesus made to us that he will never leave us nor forsake us. We also have a promise that in all things God is working for our good. Those are not just pious thoughts – they are rock-solid truths.

What would I say, then, to someone who is facing a health issue? In James 5 we read of Christians being healed in the context of confessing their sins to one another. The first thing I would advise is that they get radically right with God. The Steps To Freedom In Christ is a tool that can be used to do this comprehensively through confessing sins and resisting the enemy (and the third book in this series talks more about the process). I infer from the context of the passage that the healing James is talking about is primarily healing from health issues that have a spiritual root. Having said that, we cannot know if a particular illness has a spiritual root or not, and I would encourage anyone with any health issue, once they have got radically right with God, to ask the elders of the church to pray for them and anoint them with oil as per James' instructions. I would expect any issue with a spiritual root to disappear at that point and, as mentioned above, we do see that happen from time to time.

If the illness remains, then I think you can assume that this is not a spiritual issue but a physical one, a result of the physical decay that set in after the Fall. At that point you have taken responsibility to do what you can do and you can entrust yourself to God and leave the rest to him.

I would continue to pray for healing because God clearly does sometimes step in and heal supernaturally. But I would also advise concentrating on the truth that God will sustain you in this, will always be there, and is working absolutely every circumstance for your good. He delights in working through our weakness.

Finance

When it comes to feeling insecure about finance, Philippians 4:10–19 is a great place to start. Often Christians will just quote verse 19, 'And my God will meet all your needs according to his glorious riches in Christ Jesus', and give the impression that we can simply expect God to meet all our needs – full stop. However, we need to look carefully at the context.

For a start, look at how Paul describes the orientation that he himself has learned to have (verses 11–13):

> *I have learned to be content whatever the circumstances. I know what it is to be in need, and I know what it is to have plenty. I have learned the secret of being content in any and every situation, whether well fed or hungry, whether living in plenty or in want. I can do everything through him who gives me strength.*

This is Paul's description of what he has been through (2 Corinthians 11:23–27):

> *I have worked much harder, been in prison more frequently, been flogged more severely, and been exposed to death again and again. Five times I received from the Jews the forty lashes minus one. Three times I was beaten with rods, once I was stoned, three times I was shipwrecked, I spent a night and a day in the open sea, I have been constantly on the move. I have been in danger from rivers, in danger from bandits, in danger from my own countrymen, in danger from Gentiles; in danger in the city, in danger in the country, in danger at sea; and in danger from false brothers. I have laboured and toiled and have often gone without sleep; I have known hunger and thirst and have often gone without food; I have been cold and naked.*

I'm not sure that I would easily describe these kinds of scenarios as demonstrating God meeting all my needs. But Paul does. He has learned to be content in whatever circumstance he finds himself. How? He has learned that God is always there; that God never lets him down.

The whole passage is in the context of the Philippians having made a financial gift, the latest of many, even though they could not afford it. It is at that point that Paul assures them that God will meet all their needs.

Both Paul and the Philippian church were fully engaged in the works God had for them to do. They were playing their part. They had stepped up to their responsibility. If you are following the path God has for you and are taking your responsibility seriously, you can rely 100 per cent on the truth that God will meet every single one of your needs. He will sustain you. You will find that you can do all things through him who gives you strength.

The promise does not apply if we go our own way, in effect saying, 'This is the way I'm walking, Lord – bless me in it.' That's not how God works. He sustains those who walk in his way. However, the bottom line here is that, as we walk the way God has for us, we can be absolutely certain that he will meet every need.

In Christ, we really do have the same absolute security that Adam and Eve had before the Fall. There really is no need to worry about anything as long as we are choosing to walk the way God shows us to walk.

You are accepted

The third of the great needs that we have as a result of the Fall is that of acceptance. Again, the wonderful truth is that if we are Christians, we are no longer rejected or unloved. In Christ we are completely and unconditionally accepted. Again, it has nothing to do with our behaviour. It is what Christ has done for us.

The story is told of a successful businessman whose son was to start work in his company. He spoke to his staff and said, 'My son starts work here on Monday. However, I don't want you to give him any special treatment. Treat him just like any other son of mine!'

That is in effect what God says about you. 1 John 3:1 says, 'How great is the love the Father has lavished on us, that we should be called children of God!' Clearly desperate to get us to understand the importance of being a child of God, John then adds, 'And that is what we are!' We are completely and utterly accepted, as a perfect father accepts his children.

Jesus knew that we would struggle with the fact of our acceptance by God, and one of his most popular stories illustrated this truth (Luke 15:11–32). He told how a father had two sons, one of whom decided to ask for his share of his father's estate before he died. It was granted to him and he simply upped and left, squandering the money on a high-rolling lifestyle. It's as if Jesus was thinking of the very worst things he could think of for this son to do. He showed no respect whatsoever for his father. He engaged in adultery, spending money on prostitutes. Then, when he had no money left, he even stooped so low as to take a job looking after the animals that, to Jews, were the epitome of uncleanness – pigs. It's difficult to imagine that he could have behaved more badly, less deservingly of his title as son. He himself assumed that he had blown it completely and came back to his father, not expecting to be received any more as a son but hoping simply for a job as a hired hand, one who would have to earn anything that might come from the father.

Yet when he returned to the family estate, it turned out that the father had been looking out for him day after day. He immediately embraced this smelly, dirty, broken individual, put rich clothes on him and threw a magnificent party.

That's what it means to be a child of God. You will always be a child of God. Even if you fall flat on your face and make a complete mess. God gives you freedom to fail. He is rooting for you and has given you everything you need so that you do not have to fail. But if you do, his loving arms are there to welcome you back, no matter how badly you have messed up. That's what the Bible calls 'grace'. No wonder John Newton coined the phrase 'amazing grace'!

Yet there is another character in the story. There was also a brother, one who did not throw everything back in his father's face but stayed and worked hard. He always toed the line and did what was expected of him. If you look at the context of the story, he clearly represents the religious people of the day, the ones who thought they could please God by doing the right things. He was completely unable to get his head around the concept of grace. To him, you earn the father's favour by what you do. When his brother returned and, instead of being turned away or at the very least severely disciplined, he had a party thrown for him, this older brother was incandescent with rage. You can almost hear him sputtering, 'But, but, but... All these years I have done everything right. I've played by the rules. And you never threw a party for me. It's so unfair!'

He didn't understand that the father's love and acceptance was as little to do with his *good* outward behaviour as it was to do with the other son's *bad* outward behaviour. It is simply nothing to do with behaviour. He did not understand that grace is both fair – in that it is equally available to everyone – and unfair in that the punishment due for our failures is taken by someone else, Jesus Christ. How well have you understood that?

Neither can we please God by what we know. Some think that becoming a Christian disciple is about collecting certain facts, assimilating various pieces of knowledge – the Apostle Paul, for example, thought that originally. He had the best religious pedigree there was, all the religious knowledge going. However, when he was struck down by God on the road to Damascus, he rediscovered the true knowledge of God that Adam had originally – a real, intimate relationship, not just a theological concept. His response was: 'I consider everything a loss compared to the surpassing greatness of knowing Christ Jesus my Lord... I consider them rubbish' (Philippians 3:8).

Knowing God has precious little to do with collecting pieces of information. It's about knowing a real, living person in a deeper way. It's about relationship.

It may be that you picked up this book because you feel you need to know more about what it means to be a fruitful disciple. That's a good reason. But it really isn't so much about knowing facts as knowing the Truth. And Jesus is the Truth.

Acceptance by God, of course, is not the end of the story. We also crave acceptance from others. The truth is that we may or may not be accepted by other people. Sometimes it's painful when they don't accept us. However, the only person who really counts when it comes to being accepted is God. If he declares you acceptable (which he has) and he accepts you unconditionally (which he does), then you are intrinsically acceptable. Once you know this truth, you can be free from much of the pain that comes when other people do not accept you. It's only painful if you believe the lie that their lack of acceptance somehow makes you unacceptable. This is one person's experience:

> A year ago, I cried out to the Lord for a foundation to my life as I had been a Christian for about 5 years but was feeling like a constant failure. That was when I first went through the Freedom In Christ course and discovered that there is 'No condemnation for those that are in Christ' (I had lived with daily feelings of condemnation). I also started to really accept the fact that I was already accepted by God and no amount of good works would make me more acceptable.

Well, this summer, I felt the Lord saying that He wanted me to accept His love so I asked him how to do that and it seemed he just wanted me to believe and trust that He did really love me – so I did! The change is unbelievable. For the past 14 years I have had a heavy spiritual oppression which has prevented me from doing many things (talking to people for example – I simply couldn't speak in many social situations). Now it has almost completely gone – I have the occasional wobble but on the whole I am really enjoying talking to people – where I used to be tormented by thoughts that I had said the wrong thing or that people didn't like me, I am now of the attitude that I don't really care what people think of me and the bizarre thing is that people seem to want to talk to me much more now... I feel I am free to be the person I was created to be and it's okay to say or do the wrong thing from time to time. I don't look at other people and think I should be more like them – in fact I think I should just become more like me!

I thought I would need some specially anointed person to pray for me in order to be free but really all I needed was the Truth and thanks to the Freedom In Christ course I realised that the Truth really does set you free.

Get a life!

'He who has the Son has life; he who does not have the Son does not have life' (1 John 5:12). All of the things we have been considering spring from the fact that Christians have received back from God the life that Adam and Eve lost.

You may be thinking, 'Does all this really apply to me?' The answer is a definite 'yes' if you have made a decision to take God up on his offer of life through Jesus Christ and have decided to make him your Lord. But it's a 'no' if you have not done this.

If you know you are not a Christian, or you are not quite sure whether or not you are one, then it's very easy to put that right by making a decision to accept his gift of forgiveness and life and in return deciding to make him the Lord of your life. You can do that simply by speaking to him in your own heart using a prayer such as this:

> 'Lord Jesus, thank you for creating me to have this amazing life. Thank you for dying in my place to take away all of my sin and to make it possible for me to have that life back here and now. Right now I give myself completely to you and make you Lord of my life. Thank you that I now belong to you.'

If you said that and meant it, you now have that life. It's as simple – and as profound – as that.

If you prayed that prayer for the first time, go and tell someone. It might well make their day. It means that all of the things we've been talking about now apply to you. You are a child of God and no one can change that.

Being Who You Are

Some things are just difficult to get your mind round, aren't they? That prayer at the end of the last chapter, for example. It's made up of words printed on a page like so many billions of other pages. Yet, if someone took them and prayed them from the heart for the first time, they have just experienced the most significant moment of their entire life (whether they realize it or not). If you were already a Christian, there was a similar moment in your life when you made Jesus your Lord, even if you can't actually remember it.

The reason this is so important goes back to that fundamental question we posed earlier: who are you deep down inside? The Bible tells us that at one time, because of Adam's sin, 'we were by nature objects of wrath' (Ephesians 2:3). In other words, deep down inside we were offensive to God and we couldn't do anything about it. We were spiritually dead, separated from God and, even worse, intrinsically displeasing to him. In the words of John Calvin, we were 'utterly depraved'.

You've probably heard the old joke about the caterpillar who, on seeing a butterfly fly past, turned to his friend and said, 'You'll never get me up in one of those things!' Is a butterfly just a 'converted caterpillar'? Well, it certainly looks completely different. What about you – now that you are a Christian? Are you just a 'converted human being', essentially the same as you were before but with some added benefits? No.

The moment you became a Christian was the defining moment of your life. You are not the same person as when you were born. You may still have similar physical characteristics, but spiritually everything changed for you. You became someone new. The language the Bible uses is very dramatic:

> *If anyone is in Christ, he is a new creation; the old has gone, the new has come!* (2 CORINTHIANS 5:17)

According to that verse, can you be partly old creation and partly new? No! It's like being pregnant – either you are or you aren't. My local supermarket often displays special offers with a sign saying, 'When it's gone, it's gone.' The same applies here. If the verse says the old 'has gone', then it has indeed gone. When it's gone, it's gone! It helps to take note of the tenses used – here we have the past tense. That shows clearly that Paul is referring to an event that has happened: the old *has gone*; the new *has come*. Try looking at the tenses in this verse:

> *For you were once darkness, but now you are light in the Lord.*
> (EPHESIANS 5:8)

Can you be both light and darkness? Not according to that verse. Does it *feel* as if you are both darkness and light? Well, that's a different question – let's stick with the biblical facts for now. Here's another verse:

> *He has rescued us from the dominion of darkness and brought us into the kingdom of the Son he loves.* (COLOSSIANS 1:13)

Can you still be in both kingdoms? No. Certainly, at one time you were inherently displeasing to God, in darkness and under Satan's dominion. But that time has gone, never to return. The truth is that you are now a completely new creation, you are light in the Lord and you are in the Kingdom of Jesus Christ. Whether it feels like it or not.

Who are you – saint or sinner?

I often ask people whether they have come to see themselves as 'a sinner saved by grace'. The great majority of Christians raise their hands to signify that that is exactly what they believe. I then ask them what they make of this verse:

While we were still sinners, Christ died for us.   (ROMANS 5:8)

Note the past tense again. This verse seems to imply that we were once sinners but are no longer.

Of course, you certainly were a sinner, and you were definitely saved by grace alone. That is to say, you were unable to do anything to save yourself, so Jesus did it all for you. But the big question we're looking at here is who you are now.

If you look at the occurrences of the word 'sinner' in the New Testament, you will discover that it is used overwhelmingly to refer to people who are not yet Christians. There are two Greek words in the original text of the Bible that are usually translated 'sinner'. The first (*hamartolos*) carries the concept of 'missing the mark' and is derived from an archery term. Sinners are people who simply cannot please God. The other (*opheiletes*) refers to someone who owes money, someone who is in debt. Sinners have a debt to God that they cannot pay.

Christians, on the other hand, are overwhelmingly referred to by the word *hagios*, which means 'holy one' or, as it is usually translated, 'saint'. Paul does not write to the sinners in Ephesus or Corinth or Galatia, he writes to the saints! The Greek word carries the connotation of being 'morally blameless'. Saints are people who do not miss the mark – they have been made holy through and through – and who no longer have a debt to God because it has been paid in full on their behalf by Jesus Christ through his death in their place on the cross.

If you have received Jesus as your Lord, you are not a forgiven sinner but a redeemed saint! Yes, *you* are a saint!

That's not just a title. It reflects the fact that at the moment you became a Christian – even if you're not absolutely sure when that moment was – you became a new creation in Christ. Your very nature – who you really are deep down inside – changed from being someone who could not help but displease God to someone who is holy, to someone who is also accepted, secure and significant in Christ.

Completely new – not covered up

Interestingly enough, those who become Christians without much previous background don't seem to have a problem with this – it's those of us brought up in the church who some-times struggle. For those of us brought up to believe that our primary identity, even as Christians, is that of sinners (albeit forgiven ones), this can take a lot of processing. In fact, it can seem like heresy.

One mature Christian lady put it like this: 'I used to think of myself as a filthy dog with a white coat on. I knew that I was covered by the righteousness of Christ but deep down I still believed that I was an abomination to God. Now I'm starting to realize that I've actually become a clean dog!'

A lot of us can identify with that. I certainly can. Galatians 3:27 says that we have 'clothed ourselves' with Christ. Many of us have come to think in effect that we're still the same dirty, rotten no-good people underneath – just that it's hidden because we are clothed in Christ's righteousness. An analogy may help: when the prodigal son returned home, his father gave him the best robe to wear (Luke 15:22). But was it the robe that made him a son? No! He was given the robe *because* he was a son. We are now righteous through and through. We can clothe ourselves with Christ because, at the deepest level of our being, he has made us holy.

When God the Father looks at you, he smiles. He loves

you. He doesn't see Christ covering you. He sees you, a creation, holy. And he loves you.

While taking hold of this astonishing truth, we need to remind ourselves constantly that the fact that we are saints has nothing whatsoever to do with our own goodness or anything we have done. Even the youngest Christian is a saint – it's a term that describes our new identity and position in Christ, but not necessarily our maturity as a Christian. It's all because of what he has done, and we have been able to have access to it through his grace alone.

We are saints because of our new identity and position in Christ. In the book of Ephesians alone, in just six chapters, this phrase 'in Christ' appears no fewer than forty times. It seems to be a kind of shorthand to refer to all that it means to be a new creation, to have that spiritual life restored to us.

We also read of Christ being in us. We are in him and he is in us. That's the incredibly intimate nature of this new relationship we have with the Living God himself.

... Who You Are
(Believe It or Not)

So, you are a saint – whether it feels like it or not!

We have looked at many truths from the Bible that are so astonishing that it is difficult to imagine that they really are true of us. We may feel that they are true in a 'theological' sense or even that they are true for others – but somehow not for us. However, although they may not feel true, if you are a Christian, God says they are true – of *you*!

Here we come to the crux of the matter. Perhaps the most important decision you face as a Christian for the rest of your life is this: are you going to believe what the world around you and your past experiences tell you? Or are you going to believe what God says? That's not as easy a question as it sounds because we spend hours being bombarded with messages from the world, and for many of us things have happened in the past that have profoundly shaped our understanding of who we are, often in a negative way.

Let me ask the question another way. If God says something is true, is it true? And I mean *really* true – not just true in some 'theological' way but true in a way that means you can rely on it 100 per cent even in the deepest, darkest moments of your life? The Bible does not simply tell us that the things God says are true. It goes further than that. In fact, it assures us that God and truth are the same thing – God *is* truth. If you are truth, you cannot lie.

I can write truth until I'm blue in the face and you can read it. But it might have no effect. It is making a real connection with what is true that makes the difference. As

Jesus put it, 'You will know the truth and the truth will set you free.' Truth does not set you free just by being true – it sets you free when you know it – really know it.

I became a Christian when I was thirteen. In fact, at that time in my school in the Midlands thirty out of thirty-two of us in my class were professing Christians – it was like a mini-revival. They didn't all last the course, but many did. It was an exciting time.

But as I grew up my Christian life got less exciting. My relationship with Jesus became very humdrum. I still had quiet times but they were very 'quiet'! However, if I'd been in your church, you'd probably have thought I was doing OK: I was on the leadership team, I was doing a little bit of preaching... I was 'doing' all the right things. But actually, as I look back, I think I spent ten to fifteen years just 'acting' like a Christian rather than living out the freedom that Jesus had won for me.

The worst thing, I think, is that I was caught in one of those cycles where you do something you know is wrong, you confess it to God and then you do it again...and again – a sin/confess cycle. For me it was watching the wrong sort of stuff on TV late at night. I'd watch something totally inappropriate, then say, 'Sorry, Lord, please forgive me.' I'd know I was forgiven but I'd still feel terrible. And then the next day or week I'd do it again... and again. And end up feeling completely hopeless.

One day a preacher called Frank came to our church and described this situation I was trapped in down to a tee. Then he said, 'Do you want to know how to get out of that?' I really did. I sat bolt upright – then I thought I'd better look cool in case someone laid hands on me or something... But I really wanted to know how to get out of it. He said, 'It's quite simple: just stop.'

I thought, 'Thanks a lot – actually, I've tried that several times and it doesn't work. In fact it was the very first thing I tried!' But he went on to show from Romans 6 that if the Bible says that the power of sin is broken in our lives as Christians, it is, whether it feels like it or not. I remember going home from church that day feeling really confused. I went upstairs, knelt down, opened my Bible at Romans 6 and said something like, 'Lord. It does say here that the power of sin is broken in my life. It really doesn't feel true. But I choose to believe it.'

To my surprise, I walked away from that issue there and then and, although I've been tempted, I've never fallen for it again. It's not always that simple – and we'll talk more about this kind of thing as we go through the course.

But that was the first time I understood what Jesus meant when he said, 'You will know the truth, and the truth will set you free.' It had always been true that the power of sin was broken in my life. But because I didn't know it, I wasn't experiencing it. When I finally 'connected' with it, it made such a difference.

Living according to the truth is not complicated. It simply means seeing life the way it really is. The Bible often calls it walking by faith.

One little boy said, 'Faith is trying hard to believe what you know isn't true'! Actually it's the very opposite. Faith is just believing what is *already* true. Our lives are transformed when we find out what is really true and live accordingly.

Here is a basic truth: God is love. You already knew that, didn't you? But do you really know it, have you made a deep connection with it? For example, if God really is love, it means that he simply cannot not love you. The love of God is not dependent on the one being loved but on the character of the one doing the loving. God *is* love. That's his nature. He couldn't not love you. It doesn't make any difference whether you perform excellently one day, and mess up the next. God will still love you because God is love. Nothing can make God love you more or love you less. It has nothing to do with you – or what you do or do not do – it's all about him.

Faith is seeing things as they really are. If you saw that truth as it really is, would it have an effect on how you felt about yourself and consequently on your behaviour? More than likely. This is where the rubber hits the road in terms of how the rest of your life as a follower of Christ works out.

Because, although God's love does not change according to what you do, day-by-day success in spiritual growth and maturity comes down to just one thing: whether or not you are walking by faith in Christ and in his power. 'Without faith it is impossible to please God because anyone who comes to him must believe that he exists and that he rewards those who earnestly seek him' (Hebrews 11:6).

You probably know that a pike is a fish with big teeth that feeds on smaller fish. But you may not know that you can actually keep a pike in a tank of minnows without the minnows being harmed. How? Well, first of all you divide the tank down the middle with a sheet of glass and put the pike in one half and the minnows in the other. The pike will try and try to get to the minnows to eat them, but every time it tries it bangs its nose. Eventually it learns that there is no point trying to get them, so it gives up. At this point you can take the glass barrier away and the pike will make no attempt to eat the minnows because it believes it can't. If we could talk to the pike, you can imagine the conversation going something like this:

'Those minnows look good. Are you going to eat them for lunch?'

'No, I can't – every time I try, I bash my nose.'

'Have you tried recently?'

'No, there's no point – I know I can't get them, they've got an invisible force-field round them.'

'Well, that used to be true...but I happen to know that there's nothing stopping you now.'

'Really? I'll give it a try...'

One satisfied pike!

In order for the pike's life to change, it didn't need to summon up some kind of superhuman mental power, it simply needed to bring its belief system in line with what was actually true. Having faith is no more than that.

If we hear of a church that's doing well or an individual

with a really close walk with the Lord, what do we tend to do? Take a look and see what they are doing, buy the book, watch the video? There would be some value in that but it's not the key issue. Hebrews 13:7 says, 'Remember your leaders who spoke the word of God to you. Consider the outcome of their way of life and imitate their faith.' If we want to have the success in the Christian life that someone else is having, we do not need to imitate so much what they *do* but what they *believe*. Bringing our belief system in line with what is actually true, or, as Jesus put it, 'knowing the truth', is what leads to genuine freedom.

Everywhere you look in the Bible, you will find references to faith. We are saved through faith and we are to walk by faith. Understanding that this simply means seeing things as they are anyway is the starting point. Faith is simply believing what is already true.

Effective faith depends on who we believe in

The issue of faith is not that we believe. Everyone believes in something or someone – we all have a way of looking at reality that we believe is true and we make decisions accordingly. Every decision someone makes and practically every action they take demonstrates their faith in something or other.

Last time you went to a supermarket, you probably filled your trolley with food, brought it home and started eating it. Nothing wrong with that, you might think. Except, how did you know that the food was OK? What if someone had slipped some poison in? What if the manufacturers made a mistake in their process and introduced something dangerous into the food? You are not able to get a microscope and examine every piece of food you eat in detail. You have learned to trust that food you buy from a supermarket is fine, so you simply eat it – by faith, actually. 'Faith is being sure of what we hope for and certain of what we do not see' (Hebrews 11:1).

Many people believe that we are simply animals that have evolved a little higher than other animals, and that there is no such thing as a God in any real sense. But that is faith just as much as any religious faith. In fact, it seems to me to take enormous faith to believe that the world around us came about by chance with no guiding hand.

The only difference between the faith of a Christian and that of a non-Christian is the person or system we believe in. But this is a crucial difference, because it is what or whom we believe in that determines whether our faith is effective. It's not so much *that* we believe but *what* we believe.

There was a hypnotist and illusionist called Romark who once announced that he would display his psychic powers by driving a car blindfolded through Ilford in Essex. He blind-folded himself, started up his car and set off confidently down Cranbrook Road. After twenty metres or so he drove confi-dently…into the back of a parked police van. He may have had huge faith but the object of his faith – his psychic powers – let him down. His beliefs did not reflect reality.

Let's look at an example from the Bible. In 1 Kings 18 you will find the true story of Elijah and the prophets of Baal. They decided to hold a big competition to see whose God was real. Both set up an altar and threw a dead bull on it to be sac-rificed. Instead of lighting the fire, however, they both asked their God or god to send down fire from heaven to burn it up. The prophets of Baal went first (there were 450 of them). They danced and danced and called out to Baal. They then slashed themselves with spears and called out louder. It went on all day. Nothing happened.

Then it was Elijah's turn. To make absolutely certain that it was God and nothing else, he had them drench the altar and the offering with water three times. Then he called on God and immediately fire came from heaven and burnt up not only the bull but also the stones that the altar was made from!

Who had more faith? Actually, we don't know – the prophets of Baal must have had a good degree of faith to spend all day doing what they did. If you follow the story of Elijah, on the other hand, you will find that by the very next chapter he is running away from Jezebel in great fear and is so depressed that he asks God to let him die. It is perfectly possible that the prophets of Baal had more faith than Elijah. The amount of faith they had, however, was not the point. What made the difference was that only Elijah had faith in a valid object – Baal did not exist but the Living God was real – so his offering was the only one that was burned up.

That's why Jesus said we only need faith as small as a tiny mustard seed to move a mountain (Matthew 17:20) – it doesn't depend so much on the amount of faith but on whom we put our faith in. It's not our power that moves the mountain – it's God's.

Some people think that Christian faith is akin to 'mind over matter'. In fact it's not the same thing at all. The diminutive comedian Ronnie Corbett told how his aunt bought him a course that was supposed to enable him to increase his height as he was growing up. It involved stretching exercises and repeating this mantra: 'Every day in every way I am getting taller and taller.' Suffice to say, it didn't work! Just speaking something like that out has no effect at all on our bodies and growth hormones. It's not based on reality, on how things really are. You can believe something as much as you like, but if it is not actually true then your faith will not be effective.

Jesus called Peter to get out of a boat in the middle of a deep lake. He obeyed. He found that he could walk on the water and did not sink. He had put his faith in Jesus, believing that if Jesus told him to do something, no matter how bizarre, Jesus had the power to ensure he came to no harm. He was right – that was how things were. There is no way that could happen through mind over matter, because it requires a greater power to suspend the law of gravity (or do whatever Jesus did). Peter's mind was incapable of producing that effect.

Why faith in Jesus will not fail

Some people and some things that we put our faith in let us down. Despite what we said about the faith we exercise when we eat food bought from supermarkets, there are people who have been taken ill through eating food they trusted.

Many Christians feel let down by the church. Only this week I have sat down with a couple and heard how a minister of the church sexually abused their son when he was fourteen. Very understandably, their son, now an adult, wants nothing to do with the church or, tragically, Jesus.

Many people have been badly let down by parents one way or another. It is so easy to transfer our disappointment with our earthly parents to God and think that he must be just the same. He is not. In fact, he is the one person we can trust 100 per cent, the one person who will never let us down. Why? Because he never changes. 'Jesus Christ is the same yesterday and today and forever' (Hebrews 13:8). He cannot change, and he is truth. He has always done what he said he would. He is absolutely faithful and will remain so.

I have, however, come across many people who feel that God has let them down. Sometimes they have prayed and prayed for a situation to change and it hasn't. Maybe they prayed for someone to get well and they died. Maybe the circumstances they have endured feel so hard that they wonder how God can possibly love them.

When I was very young I believed that my father knew everything and could do anything. I vividly remember the day when I asked him a question and he said, 'I don't know.' I could not get my mind round that – surely he knew everything! Finding out that he did not felt as if he had let me down. He had not, of course. It's just that my understanding of what he could do was limited. I grew to see that the fact that he did not know the answer to every question made him no less special.

God, of course, does know the answer to every question.

We, on the other hand, do not. 'As the heavens are higher than the earth, so are my ways higher than your ways and my thoughts than your thoughts' (Isaiah 55:9). The truth is that God knows infinitely more than we do. Our ability to work things out is limited. We are incapable of determining what is best for us, so we are dependent on God to show us.

We also do not know the whole story. Often, when bad things happen, we are tempted to look at the world as if there is just us and God, ignoring the role played by personal choice and by Satan. In the way God in his wisdom has set things up, our choices have consequences. If God did not allow those consequences – for example, if he miraculously intervened to prevent every accident caused by human error – we would not have genuine free will. Similarly, Satan is out to 'steal, kill and destroy' and, if he is given the opportunity, he will do just that.

'Trust in the Lord with all your heart and lean not on your own understanding. In all your ways acknowledge him, and he will direct your paths' (Proverbs 3:5–6). Sometimes we simply have to admit that our understanding of God and what we expect him to do is too limited. We do not always know whether we are praying in accordance with his character or his will.

We can, however, in those times, fall back on what we do know: that God loves us so much that he was prepared to have Jesus die for us; that he is so intimately involved in our lives that he is working every circumstance for our good (Romans 8:28).

We have said that faith is simply finding out what is actually true and believing it. God has not given us the option to make up what we believe. Being truth is his role. Our role is to believe truth.

Want more faith?

Do you want your faith to increase? The depth of your faith is determined by just one thing: how well you know the one you put your faith in. If you knew God the way Adam knew him in the garden before the Fall, you could trust him for anything. Now that you have that spiritual life restored, actually the same applies – but, because we have all spent years trying to work life out independently of God, it usually doesn't feel like it.

There is a limit to your faith. However, God does not set that limit – it's entirely in your own hands. Faith grows when we act on what God says is true. When we see the outcome – that God really does fulfil his promises – our faith grows and we can trust him for bigger things. It's just like putting your two-year-old on a wall and urging her to jump into your arms. It's a bit scary for her and she may waver a little. But then she jumps and, of course, you catch her. Next you can go a little further away or put her a little higher up and she will keep jumping – as long as you continue to catch her!

For most of us, the area of our life that is the most difficult to trust to God is finance. That is because it is the prime way the world tells us we will meet that deep need within us to feel secure. To give money away feels scary if we go beyond what logic says we can afford. Yet the Bible tells us many times to do just that.

As I sit writing, I am watching a roofer working on my house. A month or two ago, the Lord started to prompt me to write a cheque as a gift to a Christian charity. I put it off. Then, a couple of weeks ago, water started pouring into the house during a storm and the quote to fix the roof was far beyond our resources. The Lord was still prompting me to send the cheque but, at that point, I didn't see how I could. In the last two weeks, God has taught me (yet again) that I can trust him. Having committed it all to him, I managed to get a much cheaper quote for the work and someone who was in contact with me a year ago over a second-hand item I wanted to sell e-mailed me out of the blue saying he now had enough money to buy it. You know the end of the story, of course – I can afford to pay the guy who is currently hammering away above me. In fact it's even better than that. We had a couple more inundations in the intervening period which caused sufficient damage to warrant a call to the insurers. We are now getting two bedrooms redecorated at the insurer's expense.

I finally got round to sending the cheque. However, this would have made a much better story if I had sent the cheque at the time God originally prompted! Even so, just days after I had sent it, someone sent me a substantial gift out of the blue that was much larger than the cheque I wrote. The truth is that it is not money that meets my needs, it is God. I am so grateful that he bears with my weakness and, despite my failure to act on a lesson he has taught me many times before, he still took the opportunity to encourage me to believe the truth and change my behaviour in the future.

That is a trivial example and I certainly do not subscribe to the line of teaching that says that God wants us all to be wealthy and we should give financially in order to get more material wealth back from him. However, God has promised that if we are walking in obedience to him, including obedience in giving, he will meet our needs.

Next time he prompts me to give, I hope I will have learned to respond more quickly and more generously and will not fall for the lie that it is money that meets my needs. As we try living by faith according to what God has said is true, and find that it works, we get to know God better and we can take bigger leaps of faith.

Faith is, after all, simply bringing our belief system into line with what is actually true. In this case, what is true is that God is real and promises to meet our needs if we do our part. That is simply 'how it is'. Faith is seeing the world as it is. It is 'how it is' whether we believe it or not. We only reap the benefits of how God has set it up when we choose to believe it and act accordingly.

As you get to know that the object of your faith really can

be trusted with absolutely anything, you will trust him for bigger and bigger steps. I am sure you know the old story of a man who asked a local for directions and, after much consideration, received the response, 'If I were going there, I wouldn't start from here.' When it comes to faith we can, however, only start from where we are. We need to start with small jumps and work up to the bigger ones.

In the Old Testament God told Abraham to do something that seemed completely out of character and, on the face of it, inexplicable. He told him to kill his son Isaac as a sacrifice. Abraham was actually going to go through with it but God intervened at the last minute. How could Abraham possibly have brought himself to do that?

He had come to learn through experience that God was loving and could be trusted. If you look over Abraham's life you see that every time he took God at his word, God proved faithful and it worked out. The very fact that he had Isaac at all was an astonishing miracle. Abraham had learned to jump from a higher and higher place – and God always caught him. No matter how bizarre this latest request appeared, Abraham reasoned that God is God and would have a way of bringing Isaac back to life or in some other way making things right in the end.

Would you like faith like that? Or can you think of someone in your church who seems to have great faith and you wish you could have faith like theirs? The good news is that you can. You really can. Believing that the way the Bible says 'it is' is indeed 'how it is', is simply a choice that you make. The starting point is to find out that what God has said is true and then make a choice to believe it, following through with actions.

It is important that you do not start with your feelings. Your feelings will eventually come into line with what is true, but only after you have made the determined choice to act on it despite what you feel. As Neil Anderson says, 'You don't feel your way into good behaviour – you behave your way into good feelings.'

I'm not at the Abraham level of faith yet, but as I look back

I can see that God has deliberately engineered circumstances to build my faith. If I look back to the first time I heard about Freedom In Christ Ministries, for example, I can see that the Lord led me on a journey that increased my faith. We had a couple in our church whom I liked but I never wanted to talk to them after church over a cup of coffee because I was worried they would spill their obvious problems all over me. It wasn't that I minded that – it's just that I didn't know what to do. I knew Jesus was the answer but I wasn't sure how. I didn't know what I could do apart from praying for them, and that didn't seem to change anything.

One day I was in a Christian bookshop and I came across *The Bondage Breaker*, a book by Neil Anderson. Together with another book by him, *Victory Over The Darkness*, it contains the main Freedom In Christ teaching. However, at that time I had never heard of it or its author. I just sensed that God was telling me to buy it. Odd, really – but I took a small step of faith and bought it. That was the start of a radical change in the direction of my life, as it turned out – I had no idea at the time. I read it and it made a lot of sense. I was intrigued by the process at the back of the book ('The Steps To Freedom In Christ'), which claimed to help people resolve personal and spiritual conflicts.

One evening my pastor and I tried it out very tentatively with this couple – nothing else had worked. We didn't do it the way I would do it now, but it didn't seem to matter. To cut a long story short, the wife later got cancer and was dying. Before they went through the Steps we weren't even sure that she was a Christian. Yet as she faced death it was clear that there had been a major change in her after the Steps: she knew where she was going and when she finally died it was practically with a big grin on her face. Her husband, who had a history of mental breakdowns, was my concern at that time. I couldn't see how he would survive the premature death of his wife – but he did. He didn't have another breakdown.

We then started teaching the material from the books in

our church and going through The Steps To Freedom with each other. What surprised us was that it was the so-called 'good' Christians who suddenly started changing and getting new testimony of what God was doing. So much so, in fact, that people asked us to run the course again...and again. Unheard of! Soon we had people coming from lots of different churches, and it was getting bigger and bigger.

About that time I felt the Lord saying that we should bring this teaching to the UK. I discovered that Freedom In Christ Ministries had a website and sent an e-mail in asking if there was a UK office. The answer I had back said, yes there is – it's in Geneva! I sent back a brief lesson on the geography of Europe and persevered, but they said that they didn't feel it was right to open any more overseas offices. They did say, however, that if we wanted to test it we should invite Neil Anderson over to run a conference. That just seemed completely impossible to a small church like ours – we didn't have the facilities or the cash. So we just left it on the shelf.

Well, the next thing we knew, we got another e-mail saying that Neil Anderson was coming to the UK, his first visit for seven years. We asked where he was going to be and heard with interest that he was coming to Reading – which is where we live! Then we got a call from the church that had invited him – our local large conference-running church – saying that they understood we knew something about Neil Anderson's ministry and asking whether we would be willing to run the conference with them. So the Lord brought Neil Anderson to us – and we were able to meet face to face and tell him what we thought the Lord was saying. The rest, as they say, is history.

As I look back at those events with the benefit of hindsight, it really helps my faith. I now know that I never need to manipulate events but can trust God to deliver what he promises. I just need to wait. God has been gracious enough to me to show me clearly that he is real. I think he is ready to do that in all of our lives. We simply start where we are and do what he has told us to do, no matter how small it seems.

Faith grows in difficult times

Because the question of faith is so crucial, one of God's prime focuses in our lives is to help us develop a real, living faith that gets deeper and deeper, to help us see things as they really are.

He will, therefore, often put us in situations where we can choose whether to put our faith in him or in something else. In effect, he is placing us on that wall and urging us to jump into his arms because he knows that our faith will grow when we discover that he catches us. It's usually in difficult times that our faith grows the most – things like a health scare, financial concerns, or an uncertain future.

I currently run Freedom In Christ Ministries with half of my time and a small mail order business with the other half. It's an interesting juggling act and many people ask me why I bother with the business. Maybe the time will come when I give it up, but for now the Lord has made clear to me that in his eyes they are equally important callings. Interestingly, it's in the business side of my life that I have learned most of my faith lessons, especially in the area of finance. In the first few years of the business, whenever it ran short of funds (which seemed to be practically all the time!), I used to turn to my generous parents or parents-in-law – until God seemed to say one day, 'What about me?' There came a point when Zoë and I decided never to turn to them again and to trust God instead. Guess what – he always provided (usually just after the point when it seemed too late!), and we have now spent over a decade running the business and, as we look back, it just seems like one long string of miracles of God's provision.

The more we take those small steps, the more we realize that what God says really is true, and the more we are prepared to step out in faith. God's role is to be truth, to declare what is true. Our responsibility is to find out what is true, make a choice to believe it and live according to it.

Real faith always leads to action

'Faith by itself, if it is not accompanied by action, is dead. But someone will say, "You have faith: I have deeds." Show me your faith without deeds, and I will show you my faith by what I do' (James 2:17–18). James says that if your faith is real, it will lead to actions. The words 'faith', 'trust' and 'believe' in the Bible are all the same word in the original Greek. That's important to know, because in English, when you say that you believe something, it doesn't carry the same connotation as to trust in something. But faith is not simply giving some kind of mental agreement. If it's real it's going to be worked out in our actions. No matter what we say we believe, it's what we do that shows what we really believe. If you want to know what you really believe, look at your actions.

James says we can be like someone who looks in a mirror but then goes away and immediately forgets what he looks like (James 1:23–24). We can look into the Bible, agree with it but then go away and do something different. It's like going to a railway station wanting to go to London, finding out all about the times of the trains, even all the technical details – but never actually getting as far as buying a ticket and getting on the train.

James is not contradicting Paul, who says that we are saved (justified) by grace through faith and not by works (Ephesians 2:8–9). He is simply saying that if you really do believe, it is going to show in what you do and what you say.

People don't always live according to what they say they believe, but they will always live according to what they actually believe. If you want to know what you really believe, look at your actions. Perhaps look particularly at how you behave when you are looking to meet those key needs of significance, security and acceptance. They are legitimate needs, but are you trying to meet them independently of God, in effect putting your faith in something other than him?

At the point when Elijah confronted the prophets of Baal, the issue at stake was the faithfulness of the Israelites. They paid lip-service to faith in God but were also flirting with Baal worship. Baal promised them security and prosperity in much the same way that the world promises them to us. They were really not that different from Christians who profess to believe in God yet, in their actions, go along with the world's agenda.

Before the dramatic demonstration of God's power, Elijah challenged the Israelites with these words: 'How long will you waver between two opinions? If the Lord is God, follow him; but if Baal is God, follow him' (1 Kings 18:21). It would be as well for us too to take that as a personal challenge and make our decision accordingly. Have you been wavering between two opinions? Are you ready to make your mind up and choose to follow God?

When you see things as they really are, there is no reason on earth why you would not decide to do that. The good news is that there's no one who cannot become a mature and fruitful Christian. There is no one who cannot resist temptation, get out of hopelessness, leave behind negative behaviour and past influences and move on. You don't need some special anointing from God or others. You just need to know what is already true, choose to believe it and act on it.

In looking at this question of who you really are, who you are deep down inside, are you prepared to set aside all the stuff the world has thrown at you over the years? Are you prepared to acknowledge that even some of your deepest feelings about who you are may possibly be wrong (if they do not agree with what God says about you)? Are you ready to agree with me that the Bible is the inspired Word of God and uncover some of the amazing truth about yourself?

Why not pause right now and make a new commitment before God to choose to believe what he has said is true.

Free to Be Me

We have looked at the fact that, if we are Christians, we have been made holy ('saint' means, literally, 'holy person') and we have had spiritual life restored to us. Let's understand why this can make such a difference to the way our lives as Christians work out.

Historically in the Western church, in our understanding of the gospel, we have tended to concentrate on just the first part of the story – that Jesus died for our sins. If we stop there, at Good Friday, it leaves us believing that we're not very different from whom we were before – just that we're forgiven and we're going to be with Jesus when we die. But, as we have seen, the truth is even better than that!

We also have Easter Sunday. It's not that we don't celebrate Easter Sunday, of course, but we may just have missed the point. We celebrate the fact that Christ came back to life, but the whole point of that was so that we too could receive new life in him. As we have seen, that's why he came – 'I came that they might have life' (John 10:10). And this life is not some theological concept but the life we were always meant to have, the life that Adam and Eve lost, with its intimacy with God, security, significance and acceptance. *Right now!*

If you think of yourself as still a sinner, albeit a forgiven one, what are you likely to do? Sin! Because that is, by definition, what sinners do.

The issue here is not our salvation – we have seen that God's love and acceptance of us is based purely on his character and on what Jesus did for us on the cross. The issue at stake here is the working out of that salvation throughout the rest of our earthly lives. The issue is our behaviour. If you want to change your behaviour, it's crucial that you come to see yourself as more than just someone who has been forgiven.

Neil Anderson has a helpful illustration of this. Suppose you were a prostitute and you found out one day that the king had issued a decree saying that all prostitutes were forgiven. That's good news – you are forgiven. But if that was all the decree said, would it change how you saw yourself? No – you would still be a prostitute. Would it change your behaviour? Probably not. But what if the decree said that the king not only forgave you but wanted you as his bride, wanted to make you queen? Would that change how you saw yourself? Of course: 'I am the queen!' Would it change your behaviour? Of course: 'Why ever would I want to go back to the life I had, now that I'm the queen?' You are not only forgiven, you are part of the bride of Christ!

Satan can't do anything to change that historical fact of who you now are. But if he can get you to believe a lie about who you are, he can cripple your walk with the Lord because no one can consistently behave in a way that is inconsistent with what they believe about themselves.

How we see ourselves is fundamental when it comes to how we behave. If you are a parent, think of this in relation to your own children. If you catch your son telling a lie, you could say, 'Son, you're a liar.' That is, however, likely to be counter-productive because you have made a direct attack on his character, inferring that his very character is that of a liar. The result will be that he may come to think of himself as a liar and end up lying more. After all, isn't that what liars do? The truth is that he is not intrinsically a liar, he is a child of God, albeit a child of God who has told a lie. Would it not be more accurate – and hugely more helpful in terms of future behaviour – to say in fact, 'Son, you're *not* a liar. So why did you just tell a lie?' Do you see the significance of that for your own life? You are *not* a sinner – so why would you sin?

No child of God is inferior or useless, but if Satan can get you to believe that you are, that's how you will act. No child of God is dirty or abandoned any more, but if Satan can get you to believe that you are, that's how you will act. Show me a defeated Christian and I will show you someone who has not grasped the wonderful truth of who they now are in Christ.

Someone might say, 'You don't know what's been done to me.' It doesn't change who you are in Christ.

'You don't know how bad I've been.' It doesn't change who you are in Christ.

'You don't know what failures I've had as a Christian.' It doesn't change who you are in Christ. Christ loved you when you were still a sinner. That hasn't stopped now that you're a saint.

'Wouldn't I be proud if I believed I was holy?' Not at all. Because our new identity in Christ is not something we have earned. It's a free gift. It's by the grace of God alone. He wants us to respond to him by faith, by believing what he has said and done for us. In fact if you don't believe, you are in effect calling God a liar!

What about when I go wrong?

The problem we have with seeing ourselves as saints rather than sinners is that we are painfully aware that we do sometimes sin. We therefore conclude that we must be sinners.

Allow me to let you into a little secret: I sometimes burp. I know you may find it difficult to believe that a Christian author would do such a thing, but I'm afraid it's true. However, I don't feel the need to go around saying to people, 'Hello, my name's Steve and I'm a burper'! In other words, just because I burp, that does not mean that my core identity is that of 'a burper'!

Just because I sin – and I do – that does not mean that I have to see my core identity as that of a sinner. The issue of identity is who we are deep down inside and, if you are a Christian, it's a settled matter. At the very core of your being you now share God's divine nature. You have become someone completely new. You are holy.

Being a saint does mean that we have the capacity to choose not to sin: 'My dear children, I write this to you so that you will not sin' (1 John 2:1). At any given moment, faced with any temptation, we do not have to sin. Indeed we have died to sin (Romans 6:2), meaning that its power over us has been broken.

Being a saint does not mean, however, that we are living in a state of sinless perfection: 'If we claim to be without sin, we deceive ourselves and the truth is not in us' (1 John 1:8). We are fooling ourselves if we claim that we never go wrong – the truth is that we are saints who sometimes sin.

But we no longer have to live in constant fear of God's judgment: 'If I make one mistake then God's anger is going to fall on me.' But God's anger has already fallen. It fell on Christ. You are not a sinner in the hands of an angry God. You are a saint in the hands of a loving God. He's called you to come into his presence with your heart sprinkled clean, with confidence, with boldness.

Going wrong changes nothing in terms of our fundamental relationship with God: 'My dear children, I write this to you so that you will not sin. But if anybody does sin, we have one who speaks to the Father in our defence – Jesus Christ, the Righteous One' (1 John 2:1). Your eternal destiny is secure because Jesus has paid the penalty for your sin.

Can anything change the fact that you are your parents' child? No – nothing you can do can alter your DNA. You can disown your parents or do all sorts of things that displease them. Perhaps you never see them because they are on the other side of the world. Perhaps they are dead. But nothing can change the fact that you are their child.

When you were born again you became God's child. In a

way you received his spiritual DNA – God's own Spirit lives in you (Romans 8:9) and you now share his very nature (2 Peter 1:4). Nothing can separate you from God's love (Romans 8:39). No one can snatch you out of his hand (John 10:28). If you are truly born again, your relationship with God is a settled matter, no matter what you or anyone else might do.

It's like the fairytale of the princess and the frog. She kisses a frog and it changes into a prince. Imagine they go out to celebrate at a fancy restaurant. A fly buzzes round the room. The prince leaps out of his chair and catches the fly with his tongue. Does that make him a frog again? No, he's still a prince. He's just acting like a frog! When you sin, it does not make you a sinner. You are still a saint. You are just acting out of character.

That is not to say that sin does not matter. For one thing, it disrupts the harmony of your relationship with God. A harmonious relationship is based on trust and obedience – when either is lacking, it affects the quality of the relationship.

So what happens when we do something that we're ashamed of, that we know is wrong? What is the appropriate thing to do? We need simply to come to our loving Father, agree with him that we were wrong (confess) and then turn away from our sin (repent), knowing that it is already forgiven because of Christ's death.

God does not condemn us

'Therefore, there is now no condemnation for those who are in Christ Jesus' (Romans 8:1). We can always be honest with God because we are already forgiven and there is no condemnation for those who are in Christ Jesus.

God is not a finger-wagging, 'inspecting' kind of God akin to a ticket inspector or an army sergeant always on the look-out for when we put a foot wrong. Yet so many of us have come to believe that he is. I remember some years ago leading a weekend for young people and teaching them about who they are in Christ and what God is really like. I remember being shocked that so many of their questions were along the lines of, 'How far can I go towards a particular sin and it's still OK?' They saw God as being obsessed by rules and they measured their success as Christians by how well they had kept to the rules, rather like the older brother in the story of the prodigal son.

The trouble with that is that when you fail – when you break the rules – you tend to see God as an angry figure and you want to crawl away from him and hide. I know full well what this feels like, as that was exactly how I felt in my early years as a Christian. If I thought that I had let God down, I used to spin off into the rough for weeks on end. I could not face coming into his presence. When I finally came back to him, it was only after I felt I had somehow earned my way back by doing some good things – in my case, typically by having 'quiet times', which is what I had come to believe would reflect the behaviour of a 'good' Christian. I was, of course, just 'acting' like a Christian rather than living out my true identity.

We don't, of course, need to earn our way back into his good books by having seven really good quiet times in a row. We're in them already because of what Jesus has done. Realizing that you can come straight back to God in repentance when you have gone wrong, and know that you are forgiven, is a key to becoming a mature Christian. One of the marks of a maturing Christian is not that you don't go wrong but that when you do, you learn to pick yourself up, dust yourself down, sort out the issue and continue. They say that if you fall off a horse the best thing to do is get back into the saddle as soon as possible so that your confidence does not completely disappear. We need to get into the habit of doing the same thing when we crash spiritually. After all, the relationship is still in place. He is still your Father and you are still his child. His love for you is not based on your behaviour but on the fact that he *is* love. There is nothing whatsoever to stop you running straight back into his welcoming arms.

Let me reiterate that in no sense am I saying that sin does not matter. Sin is dangerous because it opens up doors of influence to the enemy in our life. Sin is abhorrent to a holy God who demands justice for every sin and will get it in the end. It prevents us being the people God wants us to be. But the penalty for our sin has been paid once for all by Jesus. Thanks to him and the great price he paid, we are forgiven.

The reality is that, even though we don't have to, we will all fall from time to time. If we claimed to be without sin, we would be deceiving ourselves. However, the fact that we have sinned does not change our fundamental identity as a holy person, someone who is inherently pleasing to God because of Jesus. We have become children of God and that is not going to change. John says, 'If we confess our sins, he is faithful and just and will forgive us our sins and purify us from all unrighteousness' (1 John 1:9).

When you sin it's like going to the wardrobe and digging out some old, disgusting, smelly clothes. They don't change who you are underneath. God might say, 'Look at you...what are you doing in those old things? They're not you any more. Why don't you go and get changed?'

It's not about dos and don'ts

So now, let's come to a crucial question: 'What can I do to be accepted by God?' I hope that, by now, your answer to this is: 'Nothing at all!' The truth is that you are already completely accepted by God simply because of what Christ has done.

If we don't understand this, then we will keep trying to become somebody we already are! We will run round in circles trying to become God's child when we are already his child. We will strive to get his favour when we already have his favour. We will work for our salvation instead of working out our salvation.

It is not what we do that determines who we are. It's who we are that determines what we do. It's interesting to consider how Paul the apostle teaches Christians to live. If you look at any of his letters, you will find it divides neatly into two halves. The first half explains the truth of who we are and what God has done. Only then does Paul give us the practical application for our daily lives.

Our tendency is to pay more attention to the second half of Paul's letters, since we all want to know practically how to live the Christian life – what to *do*. As a result we end up with a 'how to' or 'how not to' approach to Christianity instead of knowing what it means 'to *be*' a spiritually alive Christian walking in genuine freedom. If we enter into the first half of Paul's letters, which establish us in Christ, then we will be able to do the second half naturally because it simply flows from our character, from who we are in Christ. We are not supposed to act like Christians, we are simply to be what we are: children of God.

The good news of Jesus is not about trying hard to become someone different – it starts with recognizing that you actually became someone different the moment you received Christ, and then working out the rest of your life from that starting point.

You are already accepted by God! He delights in you. He is the Good Shepherd. He is intimately concerned with every detail of your life. Nothing can change that.

This is such good news for me. Just because I'm the author of a book, you might be tempted to think that I'm somehow special. No – I continue to do the most stupid things. I remember in my teens being at Spring Harvest, a large Christian conference. I was completely in awe of the speakers. My hero, Clive Calver, once stopped me in the street, as it were, and asked for directions. I couldn't believe he really spoke like a real person... I was in awe... My mouth moved but no words came out. Zoë, now my wife, calmly explained to Clive the directions he needed to know while I was still doing fish impressions. A couple of years ago I had the privilege myself of being part of the Spring Harvest teaching team. I'm still a little in awe of all these great names, so I kept pretty quiet, but at the team prayer meeting on the last day I plucked up courage and said how nice it had been to be there with them all. At the end one of the great names beckoned to me. My moment has come, I thought. He put his arm on my shoulder and whispered, 'By the way, your flies are undone.' And so they were!

So, as you see, nothing special. But God loves me!

We so need to get our minds around this fact. Nothing you could do could make God love you more – or love you less. If you had been the only person in the whole of history who needed Christ to die, he would have done it just for you. That's how special you are!

The key to your growth in Christ is your understanding of who you now are. Do you want to grow more quickly? Well, you can. Simply choose to believe what God says is true about you!

God's character

A crucial part of this is having a true understanding of what God is like. Sometimes we are greatly hindered from walking by faith in God because of lies we have believed about him. These are often based on our experiences of our earthly father.

Some of us never knew our earthly father – consequently we may well struggle to relate to our heavenly Father because he seems to be absent too (but see Hebrews 13:5; Jeremiah 31:20; Ezekiel 34:11–16).

Some of us got the impression as children that our earthly fathers were not interested in us. We probably struggle to understand just how intimately involved in our lives our heavenly Father is (see Psalm 139:1–18).

In fact, none of us had perfect earthly fathers and all of us have experienced things that knock our faith. Consequently all of us need to do some work to bring our beliefs about God into line with what is really true.

It is right to have a healthy fear of God – awe of his holiness and power – but we no longer need to fear punishment from him. As we have already noted, many of us have come to see God as a stern, demanding headmaster figure. The truth is that he is nothing like that (see Exodus 34:6; 2 Peter 3:9; Psalm 147:11). Romans 8:15 says, 'For you did not receive a spirit that makes you a slave again to fear, but you received the Spirit of sonship. And by him we cry, "Abba, Father."'

One thing I find so liberating is the truth that God actually gives me freedom to fail. He doesn't want me to fail but he gives me the freedom to make my own choices, and sometimes those lead me to failure. Yet in that failure, he simply stands with his arms open wide, ready for me to turn to him. That gives me the freedom to take risks for him.

Knowing the truth makes all the difference

Let's look again at that core statement of Jesus: 'If you hold to my teaching, you are really my disciples. Then you will know the truth, and the truth will set you free' (John 8:31–32).

People often reduce this to 'the truth will set you free', but actually that is not what he said. Truth on its own does not set you free. You have to know it, really know it.

When I was stuck in the sin of watching the wrong kind of stuff on TV, it was true that I could have resolved it at any time by submitting to God and resisting the devil. But I didn't understand that, so I continued in my sin even though I hated it. However, at the moment when I finally grasped the truth, even though it seemed like a very tentative grasp, I was able to resolve the issue.

God is real and he has set the world up in a way that

works. As we bring our beliefs and actions into line with this, we will find that our faith is effective and we become fruitful. If we don't bring our beliefs and actions into line with it – either because we put our faith in something that is not true or we don't actually genuinely get hold of the truth so that we can be said to 'know' it – then our faith will not be effective and we will struggle to bear fruit. It's as simple as that. Jesus said, 'You will know the truth and the truth will set you free.'

There was a time in my own life when I thought I had pretty much got hold of the truth in the Bible. Of course, I knew there would always be a few little bits more to learn and there were some things I would never understand this side of eternity, but, substantially, I had worked out what I believed. Thankfully, the Lord had other ideas and took me on a journey to get the truth in the Bible from my head to my heart. I now know that the rest of my life will be about dismantling lies I had come to believe and replacing them with the glorious truth in God's Word in a way that affects my daily life at the deepest level. I've still got a long way to go, yoked together with Jesus and learning from him.

'Yes, but I'm different...'

The escapologist Harry Houdini seemed able to break even the most complex locks. A story is told – I don't know whether or not it is true – that there was one lock that defeated him. Apparently he was placed in a locked cell and tried everything he knew to open the lock but failed. Eventually he gave up, exhausted, and leant back against the cell door which, to his great surprise, swung open. It had not been locked. If he had known the truth, he could simply have opened the door. But, believing a lie, he remained defeated.

There is no reason at all why absolutely every Christian should not become fruitful. I have heard just about every objection to this: 'You don't know what happened to me'; 'My current circumstances are so difficult'; 'I'm not strong enough'; 'My faith isn't big enough'; 'I've let God down one too many times and now I've blown it'; 'I'm just a complete loser and will never amount to anything'.

None of those things are true. Why let them prevent you moving forward any longer? Here's a letter that might encourage you:

> Finding freedom in Christ has, quite literally, saved my life.
>
> From the outside looking in, I was a happy, confident, assertive, successful person. I had completed the Alpha course and was coming along to church fairly regularly, where I was welcomed with open arms.
>
> In reality, every day of my life was a struggle against despair, depression and a feeling of utter helplessness. My life had been littered with anger, violence, adultery, debt, over-indulgence, addiction and lies. I felt anxious, fearful, guilty, ashamed and worthless – a real failure. I had searched, in all the wrong places, for something or someone who could make me feel 'better'. I sat in church on Sunday nights and felt so angry – at this God who just wasn't there for me, at these people around me who were so obviously 'getting it' when I wasn't, at myself for not being good enough to feel God's presence. I sat and waited for the lightning to strike, for the answer to fall in my lap, for my heart to mend and my mind to clear. Some Sundays I had to literally hold onto my seat to stop myself walking out. Most Sundays I went home to bed and wept.
>
> Then one Sunday, a letter was read out from someone who had completed the Freedom In Christ course. Every word of that letter could have been written by me and for the first time I had a glimmer of hope that maybe, just maybe, there was a better way forward for me. That night,

I took the first step towards my freedom and e-mailed the church website asking for help. And so I found myself back in the church building, where I had completed Alpha, for my Freedom In Christ course. That first meeting changed my life. I saw, with such utter clarity and total certainty, that there really was a better way forward. That I could find significance, security and acceptance. That I could break the cycle of despair and desperation and stop looking to other people and things for comfort. That I could be free.

Freedom In Christ took me on a journey of discovery about God and about myself. It was painful at times, and there were many moments when I slipped back into my old mind-set and filled my head with negative thoughts – 'I don't deserve this... I can't be forgiven... I can't forgive myself... I don't know if I'm able to do this 100 per cent... I'm worried about what people think about me...people are so disappointed in me.'

But I was surrounded by other Christians who helped me along the road with practical advice and support and, most importantly, by the Holy Spirit who filled more and more of my heart with His love and peace.

The everyday problems of life that once seemed so insurmountable are now well in perspective and I am able to tackle most of them in a calm and rational way. I am no longer in bondage to the trauma of my past and I focus more on the present and the future and look every day for ways to live the life that God wants me to live.

I know now that God loves me so much and does all he can to keep me on a path that will cause me least harm and most joy. But I need to be prepared to walk with God – let him guide me, ask for his help and listen to his advice, no matter how hard it may seem.

I finally understand that the 'faith' that I had been expecting to arrive in a blaze of glory from above, is nothing more than a choice I must make.

I have chosen to forgive, from my heart, those people who have hurt and damaged me, and I have asked for forgiveness from those people that I know I have hurt.

I have chosen to find out more about the real truth, God's word, and I have chosen to believe it, whether it feels true or not.

I have chosen to accept Jesus' wonderful gift of freedom and in return, I have chosen to make him the centre of my life.

Nothing I can do can make God love me any more or any less, but if I choose to believe the truth, and to live by it, then my walk with God will grow stronger and more fulfilling every day.

I am a child of God and the evil one cannot touch me.

I am significant

I am secure

I am accepted

I am loved

I am safe

I am still in the Lord

I can live in peace

All is well

I am free

I have come to realize that Jesus came specifically to help those who think that there is no hope. His whole mandate was to bring good news to those who were downtrodden, blind and in bondage. Most of those people believe that their circumstances are in some way so bad or their problems so big that they are beyond help. That's simply another lie.

If you would like to read fuller stories of people whose lives have been changed by taking God at his Word, I recommend *Songs Of Freedom*, a collection of stories edited by Eileen Mitson (Monarch, 2006) and *Am I A Good Girl Yet?* by Carolyn Bramhall (Monarch, 2006). Both books show how this approach helped many find their freedom in Christ and become fruitful, including people who had been completely written off by others and who had written themselves off.

Right at the beginning of this book, I talked about the possibility of becoming everything God is calling you to be. Is that really possible? I hope that you can now see that it is not only possible but something that you can actively expect to happen – for two main reasons. First, God's character and identity – he is not a cruel slave-driver who sets you a target, knowing full well that you can't hit it. He would never ask you to do something that is impossible. Secondly, your new identity in Christ. What better start could you have than becoming a person who is holy and pleasing to God deep down inside? Becoming everything God wants you to be will follow as you live out that new character and identity and take hold of everything God has given you. In fact, this all boils down to the fact that Jesus has set you free to be yourself!

I was watching a programme featuring amusing home video clips the other day. One of them struck me as profound, insofar as a Labrador dog can be considered profound. The dog in question wanted to go outside and was waiting at the door for someone to let him out. The glass that was usually in the door, however, had been removed, so he could simply step through without the door being opened. His owners demonstrated that fact to him several times and kept encouraging him to follow them through. He wouldn't. He was stuck in the old mindset that someone needed to open the door for him.

The door to freedom is wide open to you. May I encourage you to walk through it.

It's not about us

Before we bring this book to an end, let's remind ourselves why this is so important. At one level, Jesus died so that you and I could be genuinely free and live fulfilled lives, so that we can look back with satisfaction at what he has done through us. At another level, he had a much bigger agenda. Revelation 19:7–8 says this:

> Let us rejoice and be glad
> and give him glory!
> For the wedding of the Lamb has come,
> and his bride has made herself ready.
> Fine linen, bright and clean,
> was given her to wear.

A couple of things in that passage hit me between the eyes.

Firstly, the wedding feast of the Lamb – the most exciting event ever, when Christ comes as a bridegroom to marry his bride, the church – is unstoppable. It is definitely going to happen and we are going to be there as the bride. No matter what we look like right now, we – the church – are going to look beautiful and all eyes will be on us.

Secondly, it is the bride who is responsible for making herself ready. This is not something we can expect God to do for us – it's down to us. We will be clothed in 'fine linen', which stand for the 'righteous acts of the saints', the good things that we do.

As we understand who we really are in Christ and live according to our new character, we will do acts of righteousness. It will just happen. We will begin to share God's concern for justice and righteousness and want to reach out into our communities. We will not be afraid to be vulnerable and honest as we share our faith with others. We will play our part in seeing Satan's schemes come to nothing. We will want to walk in unity with our brothers and sisters in Christ.

We do not need to keep asking God for 'more'. We have Christ himself in us! We do not need to ask God to pour out more of his Spirit – he is pouring his Spirit out. We do not need to ask him for more power – we already have the power that raised Christ from the dead. We do not need to ask him for more authority – we already share Christ's authority to make disciples.

Perhaps best of all, when we do these righteous acts, it will not be because we are desperately seeking God's approval or love (we already have those anyway) but because we are simply living out who we are and, from the bottom of our hearts, we want him to be glorified.

See you at the feast!